BOYCOTT MONEY AND SAVE YOUR SOUL –

LAUNCHING

THE GOODWILL REVOLUTION

by

MICHAEL I. PHILLIPS

Hot Calaloo Press, 2005

Dedication

This book is dedicated to the memory of my mother, Kathleen McGregor Phillips, who taught me to value and respect all people, not just by her words but also by her actions. The book is also dedicated to my sister Dawn Penso for her encouragement especially when I was deep in the throes of writer's cramp, and also for her trans-Atlantic editing of this work at such a good price for so tedious a job – free.

Contents

vi

Blank

Introduction

This book is an invitation to join the Goodwill Revolution against the addiction, worship and corrupting influence of money by organizing around 'goodwill to all' including our enemies in order to:

- achieve a more happy meaningful life
- recapture our democracy
- build a better world
- save our soul.

Man is basically good and has made astounding technological advances but our but our world continues to disintegrate into senseless violence, vicious crime, wars, devastating poverty and personal and national hostilities. Why? Primarily, because a small rich powerful ruling elite has addicted us to money and manipulated our value system.

These money-pushers feed our addiction largely by snob-appeal advertising and we reward them by coughing up the little money we have. So, we greedily gobble up disproportionately large amounts of the limited earth's resources and achieve 'money induced highs' which we mistake for happiness. Meanwhile the pushers amass even greater money, and then we pay great tribute and awe to them for amassing it, so much so that we make them our leaders. With pushers as leaders, no wonder the world is in shambles. If these leaders have ever done any good in their life, it is a coincidence. For the Goodwill Revolution, doing good is a primary requirement and riches will be the coincidence. We actively seek to be friends with everyone both personally and as a nation-to-nation goal.

This small rich powerful elite has used faceless corporations to buy our democracy and undermine the rights of our workforce because they think we are bargain-hungry dependent. But, we are goodwill-hungry more and we will fight back. Members of the Goodwill Revolution will not buy their people-exploited-bargains. We have lost democratic power but we have buying power and we shall use it. We shall let capitalism work for us.

Ruthless corporations dominate and manipulate the mass media. They bribe and intimidate our political leaders. But, we intend to

enlist those millions of protesters who have marched against war
and injustice into the Goodwill Revolution. Lets see these
corporations try to bribe and intimidate them.

These numbers are just the tip on an iceberg and represent the real
power of the people. Dr. Martin Luther King was on the verge of
harnessing this power and we think this is the real reason why he
was assassinated. But, it is raw untapped power and the Goodwill
Revolution will take over where Dr. King left off and harness this
power for goodwill and real democracy.

Our world is beset with international conflicts. Peace is elusive.
But even peace is not good enough. It is only a transitional stage.
Our foreign policy should be goodwill towards all the world
including our enemies. Our own government's pursuit of
satisfying "American self interest" as foreign policy is a root cause
of world instability. Let us lead the world by making goodwill
towards all the hallmark of our foreign policy and abandon selfish
self-interest and its inevitable consequences.

The Goodwill Revolution will mobilize the unrecognized,
unstoppable power of 'goodwill to all' to overcome the
entrapment of this money mania and voracious insatiable
materialism. Hostility is our enemy so we will use only goodwill
to spread the Goodwill Revolution. It is a systematic
comprehensive realistic plan to redeem our strife-filled world by
devaluing money and revaluing people.

For people is our top priority. All the resources, skills and energy
we spend trying to be rich we will divert to improving our
relationships with people, starting with our family and friends to
people everywhere. And not just the nice people, the people we
like, the people that look like us, but all people, including the
people that do not even like us, the unpopular people and
especially people of different cultures from us

Would you rather be happy or rich? The Goodwill Revolution will
show you how to lead a caring, meaningful and happy life without
being rich. So, who needs to be rich?

Chapter 1

Join The Goodwill Revolution
"Peace on earth. Goodwill towards men."

Why we need the Goodwill Revolution:
- We are on the verge of cloning humans
- we have walked on the moon
- we can change the TV channel from the other side of the room
- we can even use the urinal, without having to flush it ourselves.

But despite these technological and other advances the world is worse off because:
- Millions of people all over the world, especially in Africa, Asia and the rest of the developing world suffer the most inhuman poverty . The June 2002 United Nations Committee on Trade and Development (UNCTAD) Report's new estimates show that if current trends persist, the number of people living on less than $1 a dollar will rise from 307 million to 420 million by 2015.
- Communism is dead but the most brutal vicious wars envelop the earth
- Vicious brutal crimes are sweeping the planet
- Intolerance of people on the basis of differences, be it race, tribe, religion, national origin seems to be getting worse and worse
- Good people suffer and the evil prospers
- Political helplessness and alienation are proliferating
- Worsening health care crisis with upwards of 45 million people without health insurance right here in prosperous US
  - Rising apathy and insensitivity to social problems

I could go on.....

As the evil Daleks, those primitive robots of that old science fiction series Dr. Who, would say in their harsh voices," *Not acceptable! Not Acceptable! Not acceptable!*" This state of affairs is not acceptable. It is obvious that there is something fundamentally wrong and things will continue to deteriorate. So, we have made astounding technological advances but our strife-filled world is falling apart like a great Humpty-Dumpty. Even our democracy seems so impotent. All these ills constitute the failure of our prime institutions. The basic problem is that we are following misleading goals. We cannot go on this way. We need a drastic change. We need a revolution and the answer is the **goodwill revolution**!

But our society is so satisfied with these institutions and goals that they escape critical scrutiny. I will not mince words. The grave conditions demand that I must be blunt. These prime institutions are the fundamental problem for they all suck! Itemizing them:

- Money sucks
- Family and personal relationships suck
- Religion sucks
- Democracy sucks
- Corporations suck
- Peace sucks
- Good people suck

Yes, even some of these institutions, so revered, such as democracy, which we are ballyhooing all over the world, is a hoax and an actual impediment to solving these grave problems. Good people are not good. Peace does not bring peace. We have failed to recognize these problems, so we are nowhere near fixing them. But, these problems are fixable. The Goodwill Revolution not only identifies and reveals these failings, but presents a systematic plan to use goodwill to fix them.

So, there is hope. Become a goodwillie by joining the Goodwill Revolution against the addiction, worship and corrupting influence of money by organizing around 'goodwill to all' in order to recapture our democracy, achieve a more happy meaningful life, and build a better world.. The villain is this corrupting influence of money on our values, political system, our leaders, justice, the media and our entire society in general.

The Goodwill Revolution is a systematic comprehensive plan to actually put Humpty-Dumpty back together again by devaluing money and revaluing people. It will unleash the unrecognized, unstoppable power of goodwill to overcome money mania to achieve real happiness, better people and a better world.

Reject materialism, embrace people-ism!

As a goodwillie the first thing we have to do is to recognize that all attempts to solve these problems are doomed to fail as long as we are driven by materialism with its inherent inequities. This materialism which dominates our society, our world is the misleading goal. So to be a goodwillie we must reject materialism as this big overpowering goal of life. Instead set as our goal spreading goodwill by actively reaching out the hand of friendship and understanding to all people. In short join me in becoming a goodwillie by abandoning materialism and spreading goodwill instead. We have to wise up that materialism is bad for us, bad for society, deceptive and unsatisfying. Conversely goodwill is good for you, good for society and a lot more satisfying than is realized.

As a goodwillie:
- **Goodwill is our goal**
- **Goodwill is our method**
- **Goodwill is our reward**

Definition

The Goodwill Revolution is a realistic, practical movement to fight consumer mania improve your life, the lives of others, your community and the world by reordering your priorities so that you strip away false misleading goals and achieve a more happy meaningful life.

IMMEDIATE PERSONAL BENEFITS
- You will feel good
- You will live better on less
- You will have more friends

- You will have a more harmonious workplace and environment in general
- You will have less pressure and stress from the rat race to get material things
- You will have more satisfaction and less frustration

And that's just the beginning..

Requirements
1. Abandon materialism as a goal
2. Seek to establish goodwill and friendship to all instead
3. Espouse and support legitimate efforts to eliminate poverty, injustice, exploitation and things which divide us.
4. Encourage others and organization to join the Goodwill Revolution

1.Abandon Materialism as a goal
Why

- The distortion of big money
- Money defines status and prestige
- Unfair distribution
- Unsustainable unless a majority of the world is poor
- Promotes (rewards) undesirable values such as greed, selfishness, wastefulness, ruthlessness
- Undervalues desirable values
- Has bought out democracy
- Undermines the sovereignty of nations
- An addiction which cannot be satisfied
- Manipulates and victimizes us with advertising
- Divisive – reinforce socioeconomic class
- Phony happiness as we can see by the millionaires among us – pro athletes, entertainers, entrepreneurs, loaded with money but messed up lives
- Valuable diligent committed people undervalued by their pay

- Democracy a thing of the past and completely undermined by money, corporate financing
- Rich money-laden political parties have unfair advantage

How
Seek to Establish Goodwill and friendship to all, but especially to others of different race, nationality, religion etc.
Why?
Because goodwill is better than money
We all want to be happy. If we buy a shiny new car, we feel good. But, for us to really feel good we need to show it to our friends and receive their "oohs" and "aaahs", their approval. It makes us feel good and if we feel good we are happy. The expensive car is just the means. What really makes us feel good is the approval, the admiration, the prestige, it bestows on us by our peers. Can we get that same admiration, that approval, that prestige without buying that gas-guzzling overpriced automobile?

The admirer does not feel particularly good about our new shiny car. Why should he? A year down the road, we ourselves probably do not feel good about the car. Maybe we need to buy another bigger and more expensive car. Ridiculous. So, instead we buy a new big screen TV or some extravagant bauble, and here comes the good feelings again. Paying for these things do not make us feel good. We accept it, but it does not make us feel good especially if we are strapped for money.

If we perform an act of kindness for someone, we feel good. The other person also feels good because of our act of kindness. Even months down the road, the memory of that good deed will probably make you feel good. Besides, you can always do another good deed to feel good and once again not only you but the beneficiary of your good deed will feel good. Even a witness to the good deed will feel good.

Currently we are taking the medicine of materialism to feel good, but it s effects are only temporary and it has side effects that are a menace to our system. There is better medicine. It is available to all, lasting and inexpensive. It does not have any bad side effects, only beneficial ones. The medicine is goodwill, doing good. Yes, we can get that same admiration, approval, that prestige without buying that gas-guzzling over-priced automobile and other extravagant stuff. We can obtain them through goodwill. So let's give goodwill a chance. Let's take the better medicine. It's the better medicine because it makes you feel good by making others feel good. Let's abandon the narcotic of selfish materialism and join the goodwill revolution. Let's become goodwillies. And this goodwill to all does not mean goodwill to those that look like us, that have the same nationality as us, or the same religion, culture, socioeconomic status as us. No, its no exclusive club. It's goodwill to all. Goodwill to all is not just some empty slogan, but it is an essential plank of the Goodwill Revolution. It is goodwill to all that we will use to fix our busted democracy and build a better world.

Our busted democracy

In the 2004 election of the President of the United States, democracy failed us even before we voted. What choice did people of goodwill have? We had the choice of the lesser of two evils. That is no choice. Let's not kid ourselves but the prospects of even a real choice in future elections are not good.

Both candidates in varying degrees were in the firm grip and dependent on   corrupting money. The one more beholden to corrupting money won. The greater of two evils won and prospect of that continuing in future elections seem very likely.

To depend on democracy is to depend on large numbers of homophobic, war-lies-swallowing, Rush-Limbaugh-brainwashed people changing their minds. I am not that optimistic.

I attended a talk given by a very articulate member of Common Cause. He extolled the virtues of the State of Maine for choosing public financed elections and thus ridding elections of the influence and dependency on corporate financial backing. I subsequently raised the question, " In your most optimistic estimate, how many states do you think are likely to follow Maine in the future?" His answer, two in ten years and ten in fifty years!" At that reply, something inside me kept screaming, *"Not acceptable! Not acceptable! Not acceptable! "*

In the 2004 presidential elections, the money-pushers, those wealthy powerbrokers, are elated at their success and lots of people like us have been plunged into a deep gloom. They are counting on this gloom to break our spirit and weaken our resolve.

There is too much at stake to depend on ineffectual democracy especially if there is a better way. Do not despair. There is. Enter the Goodwill Revolution.

The Golden Rule

A crucial part of the problems we face today is that the golden rule has been distorted and this distortion has become acceptable. No more is the golden rule *"Do unto others as you would have them do unto you."* Instead the current golden rule is *"He who has the gold, makes the rules."* Previous well intended movements have tried unsuccessfully to redistribute the gold. There is a lot of merit to the redistribution of wealth, but the Goodwill Revolution will not try to do that. We recognize that such an objective generates such hostility from the rich powerful forces, that it is bound to fail. Besides, that would reinforce the money mania we oppose. No, they can keep their gold, but they will make no rules for us anymore. We goodwillies will strive to re-institute the original and the legitimate golden rule. *"Do unto others as you would have them do unto you."*

Chapter 2
Boycott Money and Save Your Soul

Money is an addiction

The pre-eminent reason why we should boycott money, way above any other, is that money is an addiction worse than drugs. It is an officially sanctioned, promoted, and widely admired addiction. It is an insatiable lust. The more you have, the more you want. It is never enough. You are never able to satisfy your needs .You get a raise and automatically your spending doubles the amount of the raise to keep you scrambling and unsatisfied.

The world is in crisis because of the prevalence, acceptance and promotion of this addiction. We are the addicts and the money pushers rule the world. To be sure, there is merit in money to satisfy legitimate needs and for security from want. The problem is that the money pushers have distorted our legitimate needs by the bombardment of slick clever advertising.

We have been so conditioned to money as the universal goal and key to happiness in life that money has become a sacred cow. So money is unchallenged and accepted as the "normal" goal of life. But, we do not realize that we are just addicts to money, wanting more and more and never being satisfied, never having enough. The things people do for money! We are driven by consumer mania and manipulated by advertising. We are so brainwashed that it is very difficult to break this addiction. All addiction is difficult to break, but even acknowledging this money mania as addiction is difficult. Instead we are told this lust for money is good. It shows we are ambitious, want to get ahead and receives all sorts of praise in our society.

The money pushers are the king makers in our society. They are the greedy owners, CEO's, and accountants of big powerful corporations, the bankers, and the super-rich in general. They control the media. They use their money to dominate our society especially politically. The pushers, these money lords, enrich themselves at the expense of their victims, the money addicts. As a result of this addiction, we are converted from citizens in a democracy into consumers and then into over-consumers. Addiction is the source of the power of the money pushers, so they have a vested interest in keeping us addicted and will fight to protect their turf. Money is important only because of its ability to buy things. If we do not buy things, we devalue money, and if we devalue money, we diminish the power of the money pushers.

This money addiction is curable. The first step in addiction is to choke off the demand, this insatiable demand for more and more money, this voracious materialism. It has overvalued money and devalued people. When we devalue people we make relationships with people unimportant. Relationships is the social glue that holds our society together. So all relationships , such as family relationships and friendships, become unimportant and deteriorate.

We have lost our souls for money. *""What will it profit a man if he gains the whole world but loses his own soul?"* – Matthew 16:24-28 . The whole world! We have lost our souls for a lot less. Too many have lost their souls to money –money to buy a luxury car, a fancy house and all sorts of material things a lot less than the world. To lose our souls is to:

- lose the appreciation of the humanity in man.
- become insensitive to the plight of others
- become like a robot and react to stimuli physically, but without feeling and compassion
- endure a life without meaning
- be incapable of valuing and appreciating others
- be selfish and completely self-absorbed
- be unable to see the value of friendship and to make friends

It seems souls are not too valuable these days. Money is so entrenched . To reverse this state will take a revolution, a goodwill revolution. To start that goodwill revolution, we have to boycott money and so save our souls !

Serving goodwill not mammon

The fundamental problem is that we are serving mammon. Christ said it. "We cannot serve God and mammon." This was not religious dogma, but good sound practical advice. Money has become our god. Money dominates our personal life, our goals, our religion, our politics, our values and every other aspect of our culture. It's money, money, money! The driving goal of everyone on the planet is acquiring money, lots of money, big money. We love money so much! But, the love of money is the root of all evil.

If this is so, then as the universal overriding drive for this "root of all evil" has got to be courting disaster. So in serving this mammon, money has corrupted our institutions, corroded our ethics, and addicted us to a materialism that knows no bounds.

But how shall we "serve God"? Disagreements about that have plunged the world into wars, factionalism and all sorts of turmoil as bad as serving mammon. We have to break it down into a common factor in which all religions and unbelievers alike can agree. That common factor is "doing good", goodwill. We have to become "goodwillies". We will serve mammon no more but serve goodwill instead.

But, you probably think, "Money is so wonderful" and frown on goodwill as sort of corny and unglamorous. Since we are addicted to money, we are conditioned to think so. If we break that addiction, then we will be able to appreciate the true merits and genuine satisfaction of goodwill.

It is the contention of this author, after much soul searching, that goodwill towards all is better than money because, compared to money, goodwill will make you happier and the world a better place. Read on and we will show you why goodwill is better than money and how joining this goodwill revolution will make the world a better place.

So what is the goodwill revolution anyhow? The goodwill revolution is a down-with-money-up-with-people revolution. The Goodwill Revolution seeks to restore human values by emphasizing that humans are social beings by making a conscious effort to reach out to all people and to fight against the excesses of materialism, the materialism that has devalued humans and our values. **The Goodwill Revolution reorders our priorities so that goodwill to all is more important than money, race, religion, democracy, and even country**. Members of the goodwill revolution are 'goodwillies' and briefly, the goodwillie philosophy requires goodwillies to:

1. Resist and fight against the money addiction and the manipulation of advertising which feed extravagance and consumer mania
2. Use all the ingenuity and skills that are used to accumulate wealth to spread goodwill to all reciprocated

or not, to make friends and to strengthen relationships instead.

3. Seek to touch the humanity in everyone especially those who are unpopular and different.
4. Make goodwill our goal, our method and our reward.
5. To do good and fight against the exploitation of all people.

It is a revolution. It requires a complete lifestyle change in which 'goodwill to all' and not money is the driving force.

Why goodwill is better than money
Here are a few reasons:
1. Goodwill to others makes you feel better
2. Goodwill to others makes you feel better longer
3. Goodwill to others makes the others feel better
4. You will gain independence from advertising manipulation
5. Relationships become more valuable than things
6. You will be satisfied with less material things
7. You will have more control of your finances
8. You will have more harmonious relationships with family, friends and people in general
9. You will have less stress
10. You will have a better appreciation of the humanity in people
11. You will feel more a part of your community and society
12. You will become more tolerant, understanding and less anger-prone to others
13. You will have more friends
14. You will get more out of your interaction with people
15. You will not be dominated by money
16. People will treat you better
17. You will have more self-respect and confidence
18. It will make you a better person
19. It will make you a better influence on people
20. It will stimulate in you more positive values such as compassion, respect for others

21. Your identity will not depend on your material goods or your fat bank account
22. You will be immune to consumer mania
23. You will be helping to conserve and preserve the earth's resources

Compulsive irrational buying mania

"A shine eye gal is a trouble to a man". In Jamaica, land of my birth, we used to sing about a "shine-eye gal". A shine-eye gal is a pretty girl, but the song warns that "A shine-eye gal is a trouble to a man for she wants and she wants and she wants everything". We have become conditioned with a compulsive irrational buying mania like the "shine-eye gal" to want and to want and to want everything.

Pursuit of happiness - Goals

What are our goals in life? Why are we doing what we are doing? What do we want to achieve out of life? What are the things that drive us to use all our skills, intelligence, ingenuity, passions, and tenacity in order to achieve them? These are the things we want out of life and if we get them, we expect to achieve the big "H", happiness. The more we get the happier we expect to be. These goals are the bane of our whole existence.

There are two types of goals. The prevailing set of goals that is standard for our society and probably the rest of the world are money centered goals. This means the pursuit of gaining a lot of money to achieve this goal. Simply, we labor under the mistaken notion that "If we get a lot of money, we will achieve true happiness". And this is the problem which is the foundation of most if not all of the problems in the world today, That's why I say "*Boycott money*".

The alternative goal that I am proposing I call simply the goodwill goal. But make no mistake, we are all so deeply invested in and conditioned to money centered goals and the materialism cult it produces, that it will take a revolution to change, a goodwill revolution. But, this revolution to goodwill centered goals is not pie in the sky. Like any revolution it will not be easy, but it is feasible.

Let us look at the features of these two goals, Money Centered vs Goodwill centered, Money vs Goodwill. These features are primary drives.

Money Centered Goals

- To be rich by obtaining a lot of money
- Prestige
- Influence
- Power
- Big luxurious house, mansion
- Yacht
- Country club membership
- The best most exclusive schools for our kids
- To patronize the best most expensive restaurants
- To not need to work
- To have abundant leisure
- Financial independence
- 1st class travel
- 5 star hotels
- Fancy cars
- To be able to buy for cash anything desired
- Beautiful desirable spouse
- Nothing but the best

Basically we believe the closer we get to those targets, the more successful we are.

Goodwill Goals

- Abundant friends
- Close strong family ties
- Warm friendly congenial working environment
- Debt free
- Poverty free world
- Crime free world
- Fairness
- Justice for all
- A kinder gentler world
- A world free from injustice
- A world at peace

- A harmonious relationship between all peoples and nations of the world
- Health care for everyone
- A safe healthy environment
- Consideration for others
- A friend to everyone
- Satisfaction of moderate legitimate material needs

Rich

We all want to be rich. And why not? Rich people live in wonderful luxurious mansions. They go to better schools and universities. They eat better food. The get better justice. They get better healthcare. They drive better cars. They own big luxurious yachts. They have power. They have prestige. They don't have to work. With regards to the powerful urge to mate, regardless of their looks, age, or size they have their choice of romantic partners or spouses. A rich Onassis gets a Jackie Kennedy.

It is so privileged to be rich! So we lust to get enough money to become rich and embrace the money centered goals and are all rich wanna-bees. The reality is that these multitudes of rich wanna-bees are not gonna-be. But we are like gamblers feeding the slot machine of life hoping to hit the rich jackpot. An extremely small percentage ever hit that jackpot. Occasionally some might hit a tiny jackpot which encourages them to continue. Continue we do, only to throw back, not only our winnings but lots of quarters we cannot afford, into that slot machine of life. We do this by imitating the rich, throwing our quarters away on material things that the rich have. We become imitation rich and embrace a voracious materialism. More quarters in the slot machine.

But who gets rich? Who gets all those quarters? The casino does. The already rich does. The rich get richer. The more you try to be rich, the more you act rich, the more materialism you adopt, the richer the rich gets and regardless of how successful you are.

But, where are we going? Our ultimate goal is happiness. If money brought happiness, then the richer one becomes, the happier he or she would be. Rich people would be happier than everyone else, but they are not. Of course, everyone acknowledges that money can't buy happiness, but they still act as if it can.

On the other hand, goodwill can bring happiness. Goodwillies seek goodwill to all. They use goodwill to make, maintain and strengthen relationships with all. Friendship is important, so Goodwillies are likely to have more friends and better relationship with people. The better relationships one has with people, the happier one is likely to be. Goodwillies strive to be likeable. Chances are, if you are likeable, people will like you. We make a conscious effort to value and appreciate people.

So how do you get rich anyhow? How do we get this money for which we are losing our souls? One popular way we are told is to become an entrepreneur. .Time and time again, there is this steady bleat telling us to become an entrepreneur and start our own business. Advice abounds.
"Be your own boss."
"Draw up your business plan."
"Use guerilla marketing techniques."
"Be aggressive."
Becoming an entrepreneur is projected widely as the way to financial success, fulfillment of one's aspirations and the way to happiness. Become rich? You will be lucky to keep your head above water. Sure, it can achieve all these wonderful things, but according to statistics from the Small Business Administration, for whatever reason, 4 out of 5 of these new businesses will fail. The fact is we can't all become successful entrepreneurs. Most of us will be wage earners for all our lives.
Below are some other ways of becoming rich:
- Be born rich, so inherit riches from birth
- Work hard
- Become an entrepreneur with a good moneymaking idea
- Be a savvy investor, stock market, real estate, futures, Trump Plaza
- Become a successful rock star, or movie actor or sports star
- Become a drug lord
- Gamble
- Embezzle

- Win the lottery
- Become a high powered lawyer for a big multinational corporation

The reality is that with the exception of those born rich, the overwhelming majority will not achieve riches. Some will lose their shirt, some will end up:

- in prison
- on medication
- stuffing cocaine up their noses
- leaping from a hundred-story window without a parachute.

But, yes, some do become rich, even if it is a very small amount. They might have labored 16 hours a day for five years without vacations and finally they have lots of money. One problem - *"How come I have all this money and I am no happier? I probably need to get more money."*

So the money-go-round continues. So the quest for more money in order to achieve happiness continues. The real goal of such a money chase is always beyond their grasp. Happiness as a goal is soon demoted and the new goal becomes money itself and the things it can buy. So they buy things, a yacht, a jet plane, a 20-bathroom mansion, a competitor's business by hostile takeover, a politician......

The others who failed to make the big money despite their best efforts, are now frustrated and are even more unhappy than before because they did not make the money that they think would make them happy. So their quest for money is redoubled and so is their frustration that they did not get it.

Ironically both, those that got rich and those that did not, end up on that same insatiable money-go-round. Everyone wants to be rich but the chances are so slim that it is not really a realistic goal. Goodwillie goals are much more attainable.

Qualities needed to become rich
Smart
Inventive
Mean
Selfish
Ruthless
Hardworking

Rich
Perseverance
Greedy
Insightful
Determination
Luck
Competitive
Lie
Cheat
Exploit

QUALITIES		
QUALITIES NEEDED TO BECOME:	RICH	GOODWILLIE
Smart	yes	helpful
Inventive	yes	helpful
Mean	yes	no
Selfish	yes	no
Ruthless	yes	no
Hardworking	yes	helpful
Rich	yes	helpful
Perseverance	yes	helpful
Greedy	yes	no
Insightful	yes	helpful
Determination	yes	helpful
Luck	yes	helpful
Competitive	yes	no
Lie	yes	no
Cheat	yes	no
Exploit	yes	no
Kind	no	yes
Considerate	no	yes
Understanding	no	yes
Compassionate	no	yes
Aggressive	yes	no

Money qualities incorporate a lot of bad. Money often changes people for the worse, seldom the better. They do not become nicer, friendlier, kinder. They are more likely to become snobbish, stand-offish, pretentious, suspicious, meaner, boastful, condescending and so on, "...*scorning the base degrees by which they did ascend*". These effects of becoming rich are well known and there is even a term to describe it – "nouveau riche". I know a few who acquired riches which made them so mean that they became Republicans!

Unfortunately, the rich are so imitated that these qualities have become acceptable if not admired in our society. Greed is good. This is just typical how money has corrupted our value system and in a goodwillie society, greed is never good.

So the first step in becoming a goodwillie is to abandon money. Once you get that monkey off your back, break that awful addiction, you will immediately feel a lot better. But, this is just the beginning. As you move to the next step to actively make goodwill towards all your goal, you will feel even better yet.

Chapter 3
King-sized Bed and Bacon Strips

I was in a hotel the other day. I got to sleep in a king-sized bed. What a gyp. Why would anyone want to buy a king-sized bed? Is it more comfortable for sleeping? Absolutely not! The only advantage it might offer is that it might give a wife better opportunity to escape the sexual demands of her lustful husband. It is so huge. I could sleep on it comfortably with me on one side and my suitcase, clothes laid out for the morrow on the other side with ease.

That huge king-sized bed requires a huge king-sized room. The huge king-sized room requires a huge king-sized house. A huge king-sized house requires a huge king-sized lot. All these require huge king-sized blankets, huge king-sized sheets, huge king-sized pillows, huge king-sized carpets, huge king-sized furniture, huge king-sized heating bills, huge king-sized air conditioning bills, huge king-sized mortgage and so ad infinitum and all for the sake of a nail. Sorry, I mean all for the sake of a not-any-more-comfortable king-sized bed.

It is even a lie about kings. We are led to believe that they were big and majestic. Not true. Ok some like Henry VIII were big and fat, but most were just ordinary sized. They did not sleep in these gargantuan monsters. Kings did not sleep in a queen-sized bed. They typically slept in beds no bigger than a double-bed. Hey, good enough for a king is good enough for me. A king-sized bed represents a king-sized folly and is just one of the many examples how advertisers get inside your head, distort your thinking, and enslave you to money. And what are they doing? Laughing all the way to the bank. Break those bonds of addiction. Free your mind. Boycott money!

Less is better
We have already established that money is an addiction. We do not rid ourselves of an addiction by feeding it more and more. On the contrary, we try to wean ourselves off by feeding it less and less. Just like drugs, the way to stop the addiction is to cut off the demand. The demand comes from our insatiable appetite for material things, more and bigger and more expensive. The more

we feed this appetite the worse the addiction becomes. More is bad and less is better.

Bacon Scramble

As a guest in their home, I received warm hospitality. During the night I must have worked up a good appetite as in the morning I awoke hungry eagerly awaiting breakfast. So I was happy when I was summoned to the breakfast table to join the five others sitting there. The aroma of bacon whetted my appetite and soon our host brought in the crisp brown fragrant strips of bacon. But, something was wrong. There were only 5 strips of bacon and 6 of us. As soon as the bacon was placed on the table, there was a mad scramble by all 6 of us to get ours. It was a fierce struggle. When the dust cleared, I was lucky. I had been able to capture my *two* pieces of bacon.

Ok, I confess. It is an old joke, but it illustrates the problem in the world today. The earth's resources are limited, but through voracious consumerism, we are all striving for our 2 pieces of bacon and to hell with the rest. The consumer mania forces us to gobble up more and more of a disproportionately large share of the earth's dwindling resources.

We are not   satisfied just driving a car. No instead to be fashionable we must drive a gas-guzzling, earth-resource-depleting SUV, and the bigger and the more monstrous, the better! According to the Sierra Club, these SUV's not only waste precious energy getting about 13 miles per gallon, spewing out 43% more global warming pollution, producing 47% more air pollution, and are four times more turnover-prone than the average car. Of course these big ugly non-streamlined gas-guzzling earth-depleting behemoths are not cars but modified trucks.

No wonder we Americans consume somewhere between 30 to 40% of the worlds energy. No wonder we consume about twice as much energy per person as the British, French, Swedes, Norwegians, or Japanese. America along with the rest of the developed countries of the world constitute 25% of the world's population, but consume 75% of all energy, 85% of all wood products, and 72% of all steel produced. In this way we are gobbling up the earths resources to satisfy our cravings. But, the earth's resources are finite. The propaganda that everyone can strive and achieve all these luxuries is a lie because there are not enough resources in the earth to accomplish that. With the earth's limited resources, we can only sustain our consumption if the 75% of the population that lives in the developed world remain poor and unable to consume even the basics. We are not just consumers but we are overconsumers of the earth's resources. But what is even worse than buying an SUV is buying the idea that this overconsumption is a symbol of success, a symbol that we are ambitious. We are esteemed for our overconsumption!

On the contrary this overconsumption is wasteful, selfish, inconsiderate, unfair, unethical and ultimately unsatisfying. Instead we should make a conscious effort to acquire the minimal resources that would make us comfortable and happy. Advertisers tell us otherwise and we fall for it.

Buy to impress!

So what are the advertisers crawling inside your head and telling you to buy today. *"Yes master. I hear and I will obey. I will go out and buy an overpriced, gas-guzzling, environment – depleting, ugly, huge, non-streamlined, overturn-prone, 4-wheeled drive SUV capable of climbing Mount Everest in a blizzard. "I hear, master and I will obey. I will obey...I will obey......"*

Or are they telling us to go out and buy water. Why drink perfectly good water available, abundant and free, when we can buy it? *"Yes, Master. I hear and I will obey."*

Ads suggest that we should want things that are newer, faster, fancier, more fashionable, a different colour, larger or smaller, just like what everyone else has or different from what everyone else has. Don't let these advertisers continue to play us for suckers. We must resist. It is not easy. We are up against a rich and powerful industry. This advertising industry has employed psychologists, psychiatrists, marketing professionals, and all sort of head experts at big bucks for the sole purpose of getting into our heads to distort our thinking in order to buy their unwanted products. We must buy to impress our friends. We must buy to prove that we are worthy human beings. We must buy these un-needed products or our wives or lady-loves will leave us and some will indeed. If you do not buy this, society will think you are one of the poor and wretched of the earth and despise you.   Philosophers and theologians have argued about freewill for centuries. The question is do we have freewill from God? That was the old question. It has been replaced by do we have freewill from advertisers? Goodwillies do and we have to boycott money to do it. It is a worthwhile liberation.

Fight back against junk mail advertisers

The author of this suggestion below is unknown. It was passed on to me anonymously by email with instructions to continue to pass it on. I think it is a great idea and deserves the widest circulation. So, I am passing it on exactly as I received it:

When you get ads in your phone or utility bill, include them with the   payment. Let them throw it away.

When you get those pre-approved letters in the mail for everything from   credit cards to 2nd mortgages and junk like that, most of them come with   postage paid return envelopes, right?

Well, why not get rid of some of your other junk mail and put it in these   cool little envelopes! If you didn't get anything else that day, then   just   send them their application back If you want to remain anonymous, just   make   sure your name isn't on anything you send them.   You can send it back empty if you want to just to keep them guessing!

Eventually, the banks and credit card companies begin getting all, their   junk back in the mail. Let's let them know what it's like to get junk   mail,   and best of all THEY'RE paying for it! Twice!

Let's help keep our postal service busy since they say e-mail is cutting   into their business,   and that's why they need to increase postage again!

The good ol' days

Of course, poor people making minimum wage at MacDonalds can't buy these extravagant things pushed by advertisers. Years ago people were poor but did not know they were poor so were relatively happy, a blissful ignorance. Now, not so. Thanks to better communications and advertising, people really know they are poor. Day in day out the TV tells you that you are poor because you don't have all these "things". The TV message is even worse. If you don't have these 'things' you are not only poor but you are nobody. So it destroys self-esteem. Slaving over hamburgers at McDonalds wont get you these 'things', so you wont get your feeling of worthiness back on that job. These conditions make crime and the escape into drugs very attractive.

The good ol' days were that despite their poverty and harsh physical and social conditions. People look back and see these severe conditions and blame the distortion of nostalgia for this rose-colored view of those past times. But despite the harsh prevailing conditions then, it was better. It was better because the poor had a sense of community, a solidarity, a unity. Now that is gone and it's each man for himself. And, this is the prevailing attitude not just for the poor but for the whole society.

The emphasis on these 'things' are hallmarks of our money oriented culture. Unless we boycott money, this never-ending stream of desire for material things will continue to be unsatisfied, distort our thinking, keep the poor crime-prone and our society fragmented. So boycott money!

Of course, we do need a lot of money for the sake of security. Money for that proverbial rainy day so that we can be protected in the case of emergencies. This is a legitimate concern. We might lose our job, be faced with a catastrophic illness, and so on. However, the reality is that the more money we get, the more we buy, be it a bigger house, a bigger car, more expensive clothes, more extravagant living in general. We get conditioned to a more expensive way of life and amass bigger debts. The bigger our debts, the greater our insecurity.

Clothes

For instance let's take a look at clothes. Rather, you take a look at your clothes. *"What's in your wardrobe?"* Go to your closet. Look at the amount of shoes, and all the rest of clothes bulging out your closet. I bet you will never wear half of them ever again. But, probably within two weeks or less you will be visiting the mall to buy, guess what? More clothes! That's why we never have enough closet space. Once upon a time we did not even have a built-in closet for clothes. We had a wardrobe. Now a closet has grown beyond built-in the bedroom itself but has grown into an entire room and our clothes magically swell to fill this huge cavern.

This money mania has driven us out of control. Instead of this more, more, more and bigger , bigger, bigger, we need to take back control. We need to ask ourselves these basic questions:

- What is the minimal size and cost house with which we would be completely satisfied ?
- What is the minimal size and cost automobile with which we would be completely satisfied ?
- What is the minimal size and cost resources with which we would be completely satisfied?

Unless we answer these questions for ourselves, we will continue to have advertisers and money pushers answer them for us. In so doing, they will continue to control our goals and thus our lives. And if they do we will continue to scramble for our two or more strips of bacon. Let us take back control of our lives and save our souls. Let us use legitimate goodwillie criteria to answer those questions and the goodwill revolution will be well underway.

For as a goodwillie, we will get something even a rich person can never get. Something the moneypushers hate and despise and do not want anyone to get. Something everyone wants but strangely never seem to get. It is revolutionary. We will get 'enough'.

Chapter 4
Boycott Harvard! – The SUV of Higher Education

Boycott Harvard. It is an overvalued product. Mom and pop are drooling at the mouth and straining the purse strings to send their child prodigy to one of these expensive "prestigious" universities like Harvard, Yale , Georgetown, Columbia, etc.. So to them and many others, "boycott Harvard", must sound like sacrilege.

Why do people want to go to Harvard?
1. It is prestigious
2. It is among the highest rated Universities
3. To get a high paying job
4. To be among the best minds
5. To be with the movers and shakers

Why boycott ?
1. It's overpriced
2. It's an elitist institution, haunt for the rich and privileged saturating others in those values
3. It is not a diverse environment
4. It has a very low admission rate of only about 10% of applicants
5. Many other less expensive schools will provide as good an academic education.
6. It perpetuates the money mystique and the arrogance of wealth.
7. It perpetuates the old-boy-network of wealth and privilege to get high-paying jobs.
8. It is more likely to form corporate-university research partnerships often at the expense of objectivity and the purity of the research
9. It is a power school

Harvard and all these expensive "prestigious" universities are for rich kids. They practice blatant socio-economic discrimination. If your parent is an alumnus and you are rich enough to contribute big bucks to one of these schools, your offspring may be admitted without meeting the academic requirements. Other less fortunate students must meet very high academic requirements. Even if they do, they have only about a 10% chance of getting in. But desperate parents, bedazzled by the prospect at child prodigy junior attending nothing less than a prestigious upscale school, will fork over vast sums to improve his slim chances of admission. So these parents will fork over $33,000 for college placement services, $300-an-hour for SAT tutors and $1,000-a-week for summer enrichment programs. All this and most probably junior will not get in. No wonder they take out their frustration on some poor black student who does by affirmative action. For the 2001-02 academic year, applicants to Columbia University topped 14,000, of which some 12,600 were rejected. Looking at those numbers, even without affirmative action child, prodigy junior probably would not have got in anyhow. But affirmative action will probably get the blame.

Affirmative action is under fire at a lot of universities. Affirmative action is only used in an attempt to increase the number of minority students in the particular university. University officials who justify affirmative action often do so on the basis that a lily-white campus is not as good an educational environment as a diverse one. They are absolutely right. But, often on these campuses, lack of diversity is not limited to race or ethnicity alone.

Unfortunately often this diversity is limited to enrollment alone. We see little homogenous groups clumped together in the cafeterias too often. Sticking to your own kind is safe and comfy, but is stultifying and limiting. Goodwillie students should make a conscious effort to mix with different students and welcome different students in their own group. They should seek out opportunities to associate and interact with diverse students in campus activities,   organizations like the campus International Club, and of course positive social activist groups.

As mentioned before, one of the greatest problems that beset our world is the intolerance and exploitations of the social and ethnic differences between peoples. University campuses should be living laboratories composed of a diverse student body to take the lead in overcoming this severe worldwide problem.   Even with an affirmative action policy, these rich universities are probably not too diverse. Without diversity, these universities really have a severe educational handicap and do not deserve the esteem that they attract.

Instead of diverse, these overpriced universities are often the preserve of that small minority, the rich and powerful. The presence of the poorer but top students academically enriches the educational environment for the rich kids enrolled there. Rich kids are the majority there and their bias and culture is probably pervasive in the institution. So for example, black kids there get to taste the life of the rich. Now instead of the NAACP, they want to join the exclusive powerful "Skull and Bones" club or the nearest thing to it. In such an environment, it is no wonder that in recent years we see the phenomenon of black conservatives emerging from their alumni. So, universities like these forsake the traditional university roles as agents for change, altruism and social activism to be the breeders of new corporate warriors.

I am glad to see there is still some student activism on these campuses. But in such an environment of the rich, it has to be an uphill fight. In contrast, we see a University like San Francisco's New College of California is offering something for the socially conscious, a college degree in activism. Besides, the instructors are not just theorists, but include an impressive lineup of actual activists. Of course this is unusual and a bit extreme, but a university with some reputation for social consciousness should be a vital quality in selecting a school instead of these overpriced cradles for corporate greed.

Admittedly, these SUV's of universities have an excellent learning environment, impressive   educational accomplishments and attract the best students. But, as the affirmative action suits have shown, they have turned away a lot of top high-quality students, more than enough to fill the ranks of less prestigious schools. They are not the only game in town.

There are many other universities considerably less expensive which will provide excellent scholarship and good value for money. Below is a comparison of costs of Harvard University; a state college, the University of Maryland (the 5th most expensive state university in the US); a black college, Howard University; (according to the US News and World Report) and a community college, Anne Arundel College in Maryland (based on 2005 Catalogue for 15 credits per semester).

Undergraduate College Costs 2004-2005				
Expense	Harvard U	U of MD -	Howard U	AA CC
Tuition - resident	$30,620	$7,410	$11,645	$2,490
Tuition - non-resident	$30,620	$18,710	$11,645	$4,770
Room and board	$9,260	$7,931	$5,870	

Of course, these Harvard type schools have the reputation of producing the best graduates. And why not? Just as in computer lingo, GIGO – garbage-in-garbage-out, these schools get the cream of the crop in students, so CICO - cream-in-cream-out. They received the top high school graduates to begin with and these graduates would probably have done as well at a lower-priced university. Experts agree, in the long run, it is what you do with your career regardless of your alma-mater.

So why do parents cough up close to $160,000 for an undergraduate degree at these colleges? It's not the prestige alone nor the academic excellence. It is because they expect higher paying jobs out of it for child prodigy junior. While this might be true for some fields, if junior goes into fields like social work, teaching, and psychology, not even a Harvard education will reward him with a high salary. These fields pay poorly regardless of the alma mater. Junior just won't get rich and *"if he is so smart, why ain't he rich?"*

Career-wise the expensive universities have some advantage. "*I went to Harvard*" does turn heads. It does give you that foot-in-the-door advantage. It is like some old-boys-network and not just because of its educational reputation. They do allow you to hob-nob with the rich and famous and looks good on the resume These posh schools are excellent institutions of higher education but because of their prestige, these expensive schools are sought after by, and have attracted the best students and professors. But, their prestige does not come from academics alone. A lot of it is hype, tradition, snob appeal and imitating what the rich folks do.

Not universities too! It is time we stop trying to imitate rich people. We want to do what rich people do. We want to buy what rich people buy. We want to live where rich people live. We want to wear what rich people wear, what they drink, what they eat. We want to go to schools where rich people go. We are programmed to do just that and are manipulated by advertisement. But, its time for us to realize that this caviar is just some bad tasting fish eggs. Universities should enlighten, not perpetuate this madness.

Money for research

Not only students are seeking out these prestigious universities. Corporations are too. These schools have highly respected research departments. Ultimately universities earn their reputation on research. Research is expensive. *"Oh dear, where shall we get those vast sums of money needed?"* Who has those vast sums? Of course, the big powerful corporations do. So, these big rich powerful corporations seek out these prestigious universities too. They get into the act by funding university research. Between 1985 and the early 1990's, for example, the amount of money that corporations spent underwriting university research soared from eight hundred and fifty million dollars to more than four billion dollars. These big powerful corporations are more likely to fund research in which they have a special interest. Inevitably there is pressure to bias the results in favor of the outcome that the corporations desire. This type of corporate-university partnership challenges the intellectual freedom of the researchers. With corporate money flowing in for research, the university will become more dependent on this money. But, it is very unlikely that these corporations will fund (or continue to fund) research which challenges their profit margin. They will be in a position to call the tune and bias results in their favor. Researchers are not incorruptible or infallible. Money talks. Objectivity suffers. Credibility is stretched. This has already been happening and it will get worse

So these institutions of higher education have become vulnerable to corruption by money. Of course not in every instance, but more and more, these corporate-university partnerships will compromise ethics and the purity of research for the sake of profits. This money is like Kudzu climbing all over the once pristine ivory towers of our institutions of higher learning and choking out their objectivity. The more prestigious the university, the more credibility it has, so the more it becomes a target for these corporations. In other words these corporations are going for the best. Some universities will sell out. Others will not. But, it might be difficult to tell the difference.

But that's not the only problem. After coughing up the big bucks for research, these resultant discoveries which ordinarily would be on the public domain for the benefit of all, is now being copyrighted. Yes, off limits. Corporations will extract their pound of flesh in the form of copyright fees. This inevitably has the negative effect of suppressing the research of others. The university now has an incentive in pursuing money-making research, so other research, regardless of how important, will be neglected more and more. If this trend continues, applied research will dominate and pure research will get less and less funds and could fade away.

Universities play an essential role in our society. They are the breeding ground for our future leaders. These breeding grounds are being corrupted by money. So what kind of leaders will they produce? Universities should not be perpetuating this imitation-rich society. As long as they do that, we should boycott these Harvards. It is easy to do because we can't afford them anyhow. But, more important, I call for professors to boycott them. Forsake the prestige. Forsake the high salary. Why would you want to trade these for teaching in an institution which excludes poor and middle class students? Yes, an institution that discriminated for the benefit of rich kids. Sure there still might be affirmative action to allow in some token blacks, and there might be a few middle-income students there on scholarship. But make no mistake, these are schools for rich kids. Are you proud to teach in a university that discriminates against the majority of Americans?

So, professors, break that Harvard mystique. Branch out and provide your talents to affordable universities that cater to all students. Parents too, Harvard is not worth it. Find those excellent affordable universities. Do not rule out the two first years at a community college as many are excellent value.

Chapter 5
Don't Blame Slavery on White People

Don't blame slavery on white people. This is a popular misconception. It is very important to put the blame where it belongs. Most white people never owned slaves. Slaves were not cheap. Slaves were owned by a small minority, a small rich powerful minority of white people, the mighty rich. These are the real culprits. They were rich landowners, plantation owners, businessmen, the equivalent of our CEO's, big corporations, industrialists, our captains of industry. The majority of white people then were poor, not much better off than black people. They had a hard life and during hard times people are especially vulnerable to manipulation and distortion.

Even more than today, these moneyed gentry were highly respected, powerful, privileged and very influential. They were in a prime position to manipulate and distort and they did.

The society had a good religion , Christianity, which taught them to value and respect all people, but the rich powerful minority distorted that to justify slavery.

The society was founded on and championed a belief in a democracy that held that all men were created equal, but this small powerful rich minority distorted that to justify slavery.

The south waged a war to preserve slavery, disguised as " to protect our way of life", but that too was a distortion and a lie promulgated by the same rich and powerful minority. And off to war, the brutal civil war, many young men fought and died for no grand cause, but because of distortion and manipulation of a small rich powerful minority driven by greed and avarice.

So this distortion and lies by a small rich powerful minority sucked in innocent white people, trampled on their values and most cherished beliefs, and have left them a legacy of guilt for so atrocious an institution as slavery.

Sounds familiar? Money distorted then and continues to do so now. As long as money is king, that distortion power will continue to flourish and eat away at our most fundamental values as it did with slavery.

And it continues. The Iraq war. This same minority brought us the Iraq war. They justified it with lies and deception. Did you really believe there were any weapons of mass destruction? Do you think they themselves really believed there were weapons of mass destruction? Do you really believe that they thought that Sadam Hussein had links to Al Queida despite all the evidence to the contrary? They were all lies and transparent lies.

Mark Twain said, "There are lies, damnable lies and statistics. These were big damnable lies. These were lies that killed thousands of innocent men, women and children. These were lies that fouled the drinking water for the Iraqi population. These were lies which brought the inevitable pillaging and looting not only of valuables but also the ancestral relics of not only Iraq but of our western civilization. These were lies which dropped bunker-busting-two-thousand-pound   bombs   into   residential neighborhoods.

Then the old lies spawned new lies. *"We are not invaders."* *"We are not an occupation army there to loot their oil."* No, the latest operational lie is we are their liberators. Maybe we can sell them some bottled water. Just lies built upon lies.

These lies are so obvious and transparent that almost everyone must know these are lies. But it gets even worse. At first, loyal Republicans were required to believe those lies. Even defend those lies, those obvious damnable lies. Now it has become our patriotic duty as Americans to believe and defend those lies.

Loyalty! Our patriotic duty! As with slavery, this same rich ruthless minority, this time with the mass media embedded in their pockets, have distorted and manipulated our values again. How could this keep happening to us? It was easier because the slaves were black, the Vietnamese are Asian, and the Iraqis are Arabs. They are all 'different' from us. To too many, being 'different' translates into being lesser than 'us'. The manipulators use differences between us as fertile ground for manipulation and distortion.

Being good is not good enough

Heigho come to the fair. So rather than spend my entire night in my hotel room in Garrett County in rural western Maryland, off to the fair I went. It was the annual Garrett County fair. So that night I soon found myself at the fair sitting in a crowded arena, munching on a Dutch funnel cake, waiting for the famous Hub Caps, an oldies singing group to begin the show. I was conspicuous as the only black in the all-white crowd. But, as we waited patiently for the show to start, late as usual, the people around me engaged me in conversation which was so warm and friendly that I felt very comfortable and at home.

These are good people", I thought and they are. I knew full well Garrett County is a stronghold of Republican party conservatives. I could tell from my previous visits to the area, listening to the local radio and so on that these people seemed to be hardworking, patriotic, family-oriented people. But that night at the fair really crystallized it in my mind that these are indeed good people. Or are they?

I also know that these good people like millions of other good people all over America supported passionately the killing of thousands of Iraqis in George W. Bush's illegal unjustified war with that country. They are not unique. All over the world and throughout history, 'good people' have supported or even participated in some of the most heinous acts against mankind.

- It was good Christian people that supported slavery.
- It was good Germans that supported Hitler and permitted the holocaust.
- It was good religious people that killed Christ
- I am sure it was a lot of good Christian Serbs that supported or permitted ethnic cleansing.
- I am sure lots of good white South Africans supported apartheid.
- Good Christian people hanged innocent people as witches in Salem.
- Lots of good people supported segregation and the dehumanization of black people.

Good people suck! There are many more instances so I could go on.

I am sure many have looked back at their actions or their positions on some of these issues with great regret. I can just imagine them saying with great regret and consternation, *"What was I thinking?"*

The point is that we have tended to be concerned about bad people, but we need to focus on 'good people', keeping them good and insulating them from degenerating into support of, or complicity with, evil. Being 'good' is just not good enough.

How do such good people go so bad? Generally it is by manipulation and distortion. The irony is often it is manipulation of people's very desire to do good too. For example it might be appeals to patriotism, racial pride, 'defending Islam', protecting our religious traditions and so on.

The brave patriotic God-faring Joan of Arc was horribly burnt at the stake by good religious leaders. In the words of my fellow Jamaican and legendary reggae singer Bob Marley, *"..how long shall they kill our prophets while we stand aside and watch?"* How long shall they kill innocent Iraqis while many good people stand aside and not only watch but cheer? It took good people 500 years to make Joan of Arc a saint. To many 'good people' I say, *"Break away from the overwhelming manipulation of the radio ,TV and newspaper media now and do not wait for time to rectify your convictions."*

One of the nicest persons I have ever met was a maintenance man named Bob. He was white. Most of his colleagues at work were black. But he was so kind, helpful, and willing to help everyone without exception. I could tell from conversation with him that he had a secret, a dark secret. When he was younger I suspect he was a racist. When he was younger, he was kind, helpful and willing, but only to white people like himself. But time had rectified his convictions and he extended goodwill to all men. He was truly a friend to all. He had become a 'goodwillie'.

We have to become 'goodwillies' too. As with slavery, this same rich ruthless minority would have us share their collective guilt for their horrific actions. And, they will do it again and again in the future. They will continue to manipulate us, unless we change. We have to insulate ourselves with a philosophy of goodwill towards all mankind right now, and not to just our friends, family and people that look like us. I am sure lots of KKK members are excellent family men and patriotic citizens! That's not good enough! Good people have to be good to all. That is the best insulation to keep 'good' people from doing bad because of the manipulation and distortion of this small rich ruthless powerful minority.

We must join the goodwill revolution and become goodwillies. We must seek peace on earth and goodwill to all. Not just pay lip service to it, but live it every day. As with slavery, are we going to be on the side of the slave masters or are we going to be on the side of the abolitionists? Join the goodwill revolution. Become a goodwillie and become a new abolitionist.

Chapter 6
American Democracy Sucks

Boycott money, to save democracy

- Dick Cheney was one of only two US Congress members who voted against a resolution calling for the release of Nelson Mandela from prison
- Dick Cheney voted against the Equal Rights Amendment which stated " *Equality of rights under the law shall not be denied or abridged by the United States or any state on account of sex.* "
- Dick Cheney repeatedly opposed economic sanctions on apartheid South Africa in 1985, 1986 and 1988.

Dick Cheney is now the Vice President. How could almost half of voting America support such a man for the 2nd most powerful position in the US, maybe the world? Easy. Because he is:

- Rich
- Powerful
- Has strong corporate support especially from powerful oil companies
- Able to hire top advertising companies to make him a saleable product, regardless of his past

We are helpless to do much about this and at this rate, even worse than Cheney is likely to follow. The sad fact is that the presidency and democracy have been overthrown by the king, and the king is money. Yes, corporate money has rendered real democracy virtually obsolete. Campaign reform, third party, etc., to rescue our democracy do not stand a chance against money. Not only do they not stand a chance, they will not make the slightest dent. The sad fact is that more and more in America today, anyone who is rich enough can run for political office and win regardless of their public record.

In 1996 the average cost of winning a US senate seat was $4.7 million. Jesse Helms (R-NC) ran the most expensive race of the year at $14.6 million. To run for a US House of Representatives seat that year, the average cost to the winner was

$673,000 with the highest being Newt Gingrich at $5.6 million. Compared with 1994:

US Senate	1996	1994
Average winner spent	$4,692,110	$4,569,940
Average loser spent	$2,773,756	$3,426,509
Most expensive campaign	$14,587,143	$29,969,695

US House of Representatives	1996	1994
Average winner spent	$673,739	$516,126
Average loser spent	$265,675	$238,715
Most expensive campaign	$5,577,715	$2,621,479

So more and more our political leaders will be the rich and powerful or agents of the rich and powerful that buy them. We will be controlled by a minority consisting of a mere few rich and powerful people.

This is ironic as this is precisely what democracy was set up to prevent. Throughout history ordinary people have had to struggle against the domination of a small minority of powerful people. Sometimes it was kings, feudal lords, aristocrats, rich merchants, landowners, industrialists, etc.. For example:

- A king or a feudal lord had the right to help himself to the wife or daughter of any of his subjects for his sexual pleasure. He had that right and the ordinary man could do nothing about it.

- A rich industrialist once had the right to hire children to work 7 days a week from dawn til dusk for pennies. He had that right and the ordinary man could do nothing about it.

Democracy grew out of these injustices and gradually people fought for these rights until they achieved the democracy of *"government of the people, by the people for the people"*.

This democracy did not come easy. It is a historical fact that the rich powerful minority with the rights and privileges did not and still do not want to share them or give them up willingly. Political parties originated in this fight for democracies, this fight for equal rights, equal justice, equal protection under law and all sort of protection from the greedy ruthless rich and powerful minority.

Money and Political Parties

The evolution of democracy is basically the fight to gain equality from the rich and powerful. Today this rich and powerful minority is fighting back – *and winning!*

So rich and powerful people have always had all sorts of rights and privileges. Ordinary people did not and were generally exploited by the rich and powerful, be it king, feudal lord, wealthy landowner, millionaire industrialist, etc. Political parties arose basically to fight against this exploitation and provide rights for ordinary people.

So rich and powerful people had no need for political parties or democracy. Instead they saw political parties as a threat to their wealth, exclusive rights, power and privileges. The graduated income tax! They opposed that then and do so even now. Without political parties there would be no ban on child labor, no minimum wage, no overtime pay for examples. These are examples of political parties fighting the rich and powerful for the rights of ordinary people. Once upon a time only landowners could vote. Women could not vote. Blacks could not vote.

Political parties worked to make government strong enough to stand up to this rich powerful minority, to enact laws so that the government could protect the ordinary people from abuses by them. Democracy's finest hour in two party systems was when these parties competed to protect the rights of the ordinary man from the rich and powerful. That was how it was supposed to work. Now the rich are doing everything to weaken and undermine government so that once again it will not be strong enough to stand up to the rich and powerful on behalf of the people.

However, since these political parties became a threat to the rich, what could they do? In time they have learnt that they can't beat them so they join them, well not really them but one of them. All over the world where there are two-party systems, there is the "rich" party and "real" party. The "rich" party is an advocate for the rich. The "real" party is true in the real sense of political parties, the advocates of ordinary people

The "mighty rich" party.
In America there is not much doubt which is the rich party. It is undisputedly the Republican party.
- No one joins this party to preserve the environment. *"We will make more money if we drill in the arctic preserve."*
- No one joins this party to increase the minimum wage.
- No one joins this party because they are concerned about rising health costs and the millions without any health insurance at all.

Traditionally one of the most privileged groups here in America has been white men for which they have enjoyed the economic advantages it bestowed. Attempts to level the playing field so that all might share these benefits such as women and blacks have been opposed by the "mighty rich" party.
- So if you want to fight for equal rights for women, you do not join the "mighty rich" party.
- So if you want to fight for the civil rights for blacks, hispanics or any other minority, you do not join the "mighty rich" party.

The fact is this rich party has no issues at all. Their sole purpose is to preserve and increase their wealth. But, that sounds too selfish to admit. But, how can they gain public support without real issues?

Simple...... distort the issues and legitimate concerns of the "real" ordinary-people-oriented party. With big money, they are able to bombard the media with their distortions so that it gains credibility.

American Democracy sucks
Democracy is a thing of the past. It does not exist anymore. The influence of money has degraded it and it is completely in control of the mighty rich minority, the very same money pushers. In any event and many will consider this sacrilege, but democracy has always been a nice theory which has not worked well in practice anyhow. Goodwillies cannot depend on democracy and the two-party system because they are essentially failures.

WILLIE C. FIELD'S LETTER TO HIS SON
(A parodied update of the famed Lord
Chesterfield's Letters to his son written in 1747.)

Dear Son,
       I must confess that I was filled with
dismay and deep sadness to learn that you
were running for political office. Politics
has always been, and in these times especially
so, a most perilous journey fraught with
deception, treachery, and betrayal. Since I
know that you are a most resolute person and
I will be unable to persuade you to change
your mind, I will give you some advice which
could improve your very slim chance of success.
       First and foremost, your black skin,
though an excellent protection from the sun's
ultraviolet rays, is a distinct political
liability, one which I have serious doubts
that you can overcome. Even in the most liberal
of times, blacks running for office here who
had to depend on a majority who did not
share their skin color regardless of the black
candidates' credentials, imposing record and
astounding merits, usually were rejected at the
polls. So son, despite what you might hear to
the contrary, "Our time has not yet come."
Although I have taught you to be proud of your
black skin, your political success will depend on
how well yon can hide this from the voting
masses.
       Everywhere I go I see the smiling visage
of political candidates on TV, assorted
newspapers, billboards, even on posters staked in
verdant pastures among contented cows. Forsake
this folly. Then some voters might not realize
that you are black. So shun cameras but get your
name in and on everything. But don't let them
refer to you as Willie anymore. Bill's better.
"What's in a name?" A lot. Recently the
voters of the state of Illinois, to the

great consternation of many traditional
Democrats, selected an assortment of Larouche
Democrats and analysts contend that a
substantial basis for such a selection was the
waspish names of the Larouches as opposed to
the ethnic sounding ones of the others.

Of course, it is of considerable importance
how issues are handled. Let us take a
hypothetical situation. Your opponent is
proposing that every black male child upon
attaining the age of thirteen should have his
right eye surgically removed. I am positive
that you would respond to this with passionate
denunciation as inhuman, racist, and barbaric.
Even though you would be absolutely right in your
characterization, you would have employed a most
useless and impotent tactic. In a society in
which there is public approval and even
admiration for the overthrow of elected
government (Nicaragua), invasion of sovereign
states and the bedroom, contempt and defiance of
international law, friendly cooperation with a
genocidal racist minority regime (South
Africa), and the degradation of civil, women's
and consumer rights, that would most assuredly be
ineffective. The course of action to take
appropriate for these unfortunate times, my
son, would be quite different. Instead, you
would point out very calmly that such a
proposal is fiscally irresponsible as it would
incur great expense, could make the government
vulnerable to huge liability payments in the
event of surgical malpractice and thus place
a most unwelcome burden on the taxpayer.

So son, a convincing pretense of apathy
towards civil rights and such meaningful issues
is essential. Do not shun them entirely but
keep a stock of vague ambiguous proclamations
in readiness. Do not be misled by the many other
black candidates who champion such causes and
with great. vigour, justified outrage and
eloquence. Such righteous causes only

embarrasses, infuriates and incites more and more voters to rush out and register friends and relations to make sure such a person never gets elected. I was bemused by the irony of the recent Renquist hearings and the futile attempts to reject him. His opponents had no chance because what they depicted as his history of bias and prejudice to many was seen as distinguished badges of honour and excellent qualifications for the office.

As the media, the newspapers in particular, is of considerable importance to the making and breaking of a political candidate, their support is most beneficial. Do not delude yourself into thinking that you have the remotest chance of obtaining such support. I still find it most astonishing that many persons in your position have the delusion that the newspaper will treat them fairly. Such misguided optimism is the demise of many a good- politician. Even if you have an outstanding unblemished record they will see it as a challenge to sully it. If they can't find anything else, they will pick on the fact that you have a broken nail on your right pinkie finger and harp on it so often that the conditioned voter will come to consider that to be a critical criterion for the office. The most you can hope for is that the media consider your chances of winning so poor that they ignore you completely. Then you might have a chance.

Finally, son, I play not the role of cynic nor do I want to dampen your enthusiasm, but I hate to see your youthful idealism, an exceedingly rare quality today, founder on the harsh jagged rocks of reality. It might actually be better to withdraw, throw your support, discrete support mind you, behind some trusted white ally who has a better chance of winning provided that the voting public does not find out that he too

```
stands    for    equality,    true    justice    and
respect     for     law     both     national     and
international.
     'Til  I  see  you  again,  be  of  good  cheer
and  if  you  continue  I  hope  my  insight  and
observations  will  be  of  some  benefit.
                    I  remain,
                    Your  admiring  Dad.
```

This letter was written by me over twenty years ago during the Ronald Reagan presidency. Democracy has gotten a lot worse since then.

Democracy divides and polarizes people

As I mentioned several times before, one of the worst problems the entire world faces is the polarization of the world based on differences such as race, ethnicity, national origin, religion and so on. Democracy makes that problem worse by polarizing people along political party lines and often with no less hostility than these other differences. These political differences often run deeper because they will even separate friends and families.

In Jamaica in some areas whole communities are physically divided on the basis of political allegiance and wage virtual war with each other resulting in death, destruction and violence so much so that emergency police stations have to be set up between them. Jamaica is not unique as all over the world, national elections take place in an atmosphere of violence, terror, deaths and destruction.

All over the world political parties are aligning themselves with the ethnic, racial and other differences that separate us to make the divisions worse. When freedom and democracy finally came to India, the first thing they did was to split into India and Pakistan on the basis of religious differences. When democracy kicked communism out of Yugoslavia, the polarization of the people brought the horrors of ethnic cleansing .

One notable exception – South Africa.

Democracy creates cult-like following

Democracy is capable of creating cult like followings in their allegiances with disastrous consequences. Such followers will vote for and support with great passion their leader even though their leader pursues a policy that will victimize or has victimized them. For instance:

In Liberia, orphans of murdered parents were known to chant, *"You killed my ma. You killed my pa. I'll vote for you!"*

In recent US elections:

- people without health insurance voted against the candidate who promised them health coverage
- underpaid people voted for the candidate who campaigned against the living wage
- mothers and fathers who saw their sons or daughters killed or maimed in the illegal Iraq war, a war based on Bush lies, voted for Bush

"You killed my son. You killed my daughter. I'll vote for you."

"You killed my ma. You killed my pa. I'll vote for you."

Voting is not a right

Do you realize that in our American democracy Americans have no constitutional right to vote.

Any citizen who has committed a felony does not have the right to vote in 14 states. Regardless of whether they have paid their debt to society and served their time and have even become model citizens and a credit to their community – they are deprived of their right to vote forever.

Citizens of the capital of the United States of America, Washington DC, do not have the right to vote for a US senator or congressman. How ironic it is that the USA is probably the greatest proponent of democracy, but there is no democracy in its heart, Washington DC. They do have the right to vote for a mayor and city council but they are pretty much toothless as they cannot raise taxes, enact new laws, and carry on similar city responsibilities without the approval of the US congress. Specifically it is ruled by special congressional committee lead by a chairman who rules the city like a despot. He is not answerable to the DC residents often making decisions totally against the wishes   of   the   residents.

Recently they really stuck it to DC by revoking a DC law outlawing the selling and ownership of AK47 assault rifles. For another example of their domination, in recent years, the city conducted a referendum at great expense, on the legalisation of marijuana. The outcome? We will never know. The city was forbidden by the US Congress to even reveal the results of the referendum much less do anything about it! Make no mistake, Washington DC is a colony. There is no legitimate democracy there. It is a shameless fraud. The license tags of DC automobiles do not say *"Taxation without representation"* for nothing.

Democracy   can   be   subverted   by   the   ruthless
In many countries, democracy is vulnerable to a ruthless opposition. In countries like Haiti, Venezuela, Guyana and Jamaica, opposition seek to create constant unceasing turmoil and unrest in order to make the country ungovernable. This worked to overthrow democracy in Haiti in 2004.

Right here in America, democracy has been subverted by the ruthless. People have been systematically deprived of their rights to vote and the majority of Americans could not care less because it helped their man get elected. A brand new way to subvert democracy is called voter suppression. In the US presidential elections of 2000 and 2004, this developed into a very effective tool for the subversion of democracy particularly in Florida and Ohio. Simply keep the voters away from the polls by:

- Falsely classifying thousands as felons so that they would be ineligible to vote
- Deliberately reducing the voting machines in selected areas decided by statistical analysis beforehand so that thousands of voters are forced to wait for up to 10 hours to vote.
- Using suspect voting machines without a verifiable paper trail which were bought from a know supporter of one of the candidates, machines of which some went on to report more votes than were actually cast
- Using "official" fliers to deliberately direct thousand of voters to the wrong polling places.

Misinformed electorate
The success of democracy is dependent on an informed electorate. Media talk show propagandists and a biased press make

sure that a large percentage of our electorate is misinformed. That is why according to a poll conducted by the Washington Post, nearly seven in 10 Americans still believed that ousted Iraqi leader Saddam Hussein was personally involved in the Sept. 11 attacks over two years after the attacks took place. These media propagandists that are deliberately misinforming the electorate are obviously undermining democracy, but they enjoy enormous salaries, prestige and great public popularity for their misdeeds.

Only 30% of the people vote

More and more people don't even believe in democracy. If they did they would vote but typically in elections here in America only 30% of the people vote. People don't believe their vote matters. If they believe that then they don't believe democracy works.

Negative campaign prevails

These democratic political races are not to the honest, the most capable, the fair, the compassionate and the just. Those races are more likely to the rich, the ruthless, the cunning, and the ones with the best spin doctors money can buy. Instead of rational open-minded debate on the most crucial of issues, we often get partisanship, distortion, emotionalism , flag waving and downright lies the deciding factors. Why fight fair and lose when you can fight dirty and win?

May the best man win. I don't think so. Elections usually boil down to the lesser of two evils. The best man does not stand a chance and does not even dare to run. The reality is that merit has less and less with the election of candidates. For example, for the highest elected position in the land, the president of the United States of America, we have two candidates.

Candidate A has dedicated his entire life to protecting the consumer.

Candidate B inherited great wealth and power, has probably not worked a day in his life and has been an advocate for the rich and powerful corporations.

Which would you select? The American people made their selection. They selected Candidate B, George Bush. They rejected Candidate A, Ralph Nader, and decisively.

Is it surprising that people do not respect politicians? They are perceived as dishonest, ruthless and completely lacking in integrity. Unfortunately too often all politicians get lumped together in this category. But, there are good politicians, who are dedicated to serving the people fairly instead of selling out to moneyed interests. They stand on principle and because of this they are more vulnerable to the well-heeled dirty-dealing disreputable politician. But, the politicians are not to blame. It is the system that penalizes good politicians and rewards the bad that deserves the blame. And, that system is the democratic system.

Tyranny of the majority

Swiss-born French philosopher Jean-Jacques Rousseau warned about democracy degenerating into the tyranny of the majority. Our American democracy has moved or is fast moving in that direction. In America today, we see more and more the Republican Party appeals to the white majority by scapegoating Arab-Americans, blacks, latinos, immigrants, the poor and even women. Of course this is quite subtle and at the same time they pretend otherwise, paying a lot of lip service to diversity. Nowhere was this more evident than in 1994 when the impressive victory of the Republican Party in national elections was due to the support of the now famous angry white men. Newsweek reported that 68 percent of white males voted Republican. White males overwhelmingly swept the Republicans into the U.S. Congress, governor races, and state houses. The white male vote caused one of the greatest political landslides in American electoral history. It worked then. It continues to work now and is a bastion of the winning Republican Party strategy.

Of course this is not unique to American democracy. It is typical and even worse all over the world. Historically, when we look back at the advent of democracy to colonial India. the country split asunder on religious differences into Muslim Pakistan and Hindu India.

Alternative to democracy

"So if democracy is so bad what do you propose that is better?" My answer is that I have none but it does not matter. If we got the best minds in the world to devise a new political system that overcame these glaring problems of democracy, it would not matter. That is because regardless of how good the new system

would be, it would not be accepted. If that new system was good then it would not permit the domination of the election process by the money pushers. But the acceptance of the new system would depend on the approval and support of this very same group. Not only would they not give their approval and support, but they would fight it tooth and nail with all the power they could muster.

So an alternative system would be for academic purposes only. Even without the opposition of the money pushers, democracy is so revered that any alternate system would not receive serious consideration and even if it did, implementation would take centuries. That is the reality so attempts to find a better system than democracy are a waste of time.

The democratic political system like most of our other institutions, has become so corrupted by money that it is no longer part of the solution to the ills of our society, but it is a big part of the problem. It has become a red herring used to give people the illusion that they have the power. The fact is that the current democracy is keeping us powerless. People do have the power to make positive change but not by the present toothless money-serving democracy.

The answer is a revolution, the goodwill revolution, a personal commitment to the goodwill revolution, a personal commitment to the down-with-money-up-with- people revolution. The Goodwill revolution uses cultural change to make political change. It will take the Goodwill Revolution to rescue democracy.

Chapter 7
Goodness of man

Good or Bad

Philosophers have long pondered the nature of man. Is he good or bad? Fundamental to the goodwill revolution is the conviction that people are basically good. Why else do we care about things like fairness and justice. We do not want justice only for our relatives and friends, we want justice for all. We do not want to see people suffer, go hungry. The homeless beggar in the street with his sign *"Will work for food"* touches us deeply. We might not do anything about it , but we wish we could. Why? Because we are basically good and do care about others.

We care about people we don't know and people who don't even exist. We go to the movies and care for the plight of the make-believe hero. So, we love happy endings, because in happy endings good usually triumphs, or the homeless person gets fed, or the sick person is healed or justice prevails. We do not just want these good things in the movies, but we hunger for them in our lives. And very important, we are not selfish to want good things just for ourselves, but by our very nature, we want them for all.

Conversely, we despise and hate evil. Because we are basically good, evil goes against the grain. Even the robber probably does not want to rob. Even the 9-11 terrorists probably did not really want to murder those hundreds of innocent people in the World Trade Center. Even George Bush did not want to kill those thousands of innocent Iraqi men, women and children. Before or after these acts, the perpetrators are compelled to justify their horrible actions. In so doing, they are saying these horrible acts are really good because of this or that reason. Why do they have to? Because, they don't want good people to despise them. They don't want good people to consider them evil. It is a recognition that we are good and the primacy of this good nature which must be satisfied. The bottom line is not only do we not want to do bad things, but we also do not want to be perceived as doing bad things. So I believe that Israelis and Palestinians, Hindus and Muslims, Irish Catholics and Protestants, Tutsis and Hutus, and many other bitter antagonists that imperil our world today, do not really want to kill each other. It is unnatural.

Conscience

Doing an evil deed is not just clear sailing. Before we can do it, we must contend with our basic instinct which tells us not to do it, our conscience. Unfortunately, conscience does not have veto power, and so it can be overcome. And even after overcoming conscience and committing the dastardly deed, human nature runs into more opposition from remorse and guilt. But alas, these instincts for good are not indestructible and like the UN can be rendered completely irrelevant and killed. But their very existence is another bit of evidence that mankind is basically good.

If man is so good, why does evil prosper? Because we have lost our way. We have abandoned goodwill to follow money, materialism and power. This money, materialism and power has corrupted the goodness of man.

Tapping Goodwill

We still feel inside a sense of outrage when we see injustice, but we do nothing about it. We still feel a compassion for genuine poverty misery and misfortune in others, but we do nothing about it. So at a movie, we are moved by a touching and moving make-believe story. This fake story might even be better than reality because we do not have to do anything about it. And, that's the problem, which makes us want to even deny our feelings of goodwill, or to fight against them. We deny them and try to embrace apathy, insensitivity, because we feel helplessness to do anything about it. Why bother?

So this natural force to do good within us is suppressed. It is relatively dormant, but it is still there waiting to be released.

Don't fight that feeling of goodwill. Let's liberate it. The goodwill revolution taps into that goodness of man. It is a source of power. It is that source of power which waged the greatest revolution in American history and won against tremendous odds. And I do not mean the revolution against the British. No, it was a revolution that pitted ordinary people armed and united by goodwill against unjust laws, against police terror, violent mobs, even vicious dogs, a most formidable enemy indeed. It was the civil rights revolution of the sixties. Black and white people of goodwill fought together against segregation. Black and white people united by goodwill died together against segregation. Black and white people of goodwill fought against a system that denied black people basic civil rights. White people of goodwill fought against a system that bestowed upon them a wide assortment of special privileges. They endured violence and insults of others of their own privileged white kith and kin to join with blacks in the fight.

The good news is that in this new goodwill revolution, we will not have to face the perils that the battle of the sixties required. Different times require different methods. This new goodwill revolution is unstoppable. It will be a tough battle but it will place no one at risk of any physical harm or arrest.

In South Africa, Nelson Mandela was jailed for 26 years. He witnessed the brutality and oppression of his people for decades in which they were treated like dogs, herded in their own land like cattle, denied even the status of human beings because they were black and a slew of other vicious repressions. But they overcame it. The goodness of man was a source of power for this liberation and the peaceful transition of South Africa from these horrors of apartheid. In the words of Nelson Mandela, in his farewell speech from Parliament, *"Historical enemies succeeded in negotiating a peaceful transition from apartheid to democracy because we were prepared to accept the inherent goodness in the other"*.

Chapter 8
Goodwillie to the Rescue of Relationships

Goodwillie – What's in a name?

One of the aims of the Goodwill Revolution is to make it so benevolent that it will have no detractors. Impossible dream. Of course, there will be detractors. I anticipate that these detractors would deride the members of the Goodwill Revolution, by calling us 'goodwillies'. We have beaten them to the punch by calling ourselves that. Just as Johnny Cash in "A boy Named Sue", we will make that name earn respect and mean something to be proud of. Besides goodwill and goodwillie just go together.

Goals

Goodwillies seek to be less dependent on money, lots of friends, a warm friendly, fair and just environment, and a better world. To obtain lots of friends we need to improve our relationships with others. In our present society, relationships between people are generally bad. This is because they have been trivialized and treated as unimportant. The main focus of the Goodwill Revolution is to use goodwill to improve and strengthen all sorts of relationships between people.

In simplest terms this goal is to become friends to everyone. We want to be friends with our spouses, our relatives, our neighbors, our co-workers, people we do not even know, people who do not even want to be friends with us, or as I said before everyone, the world.

Now I have heard many a motivational speaker, respected psychologists and similar professionals advise the opposite. These motivational speakers started off wrong anyhow. It seems that they always begin with some personal rags-to-riches story of their life that they are passing on and how they did it. So success to them is achieving these riches from rags. They have a lot of good advice but unfortunately they are reinforcing this money mania. Their message is not goodwill to *all* but to some, a *select few*. They want us to collect only the 'nice' people, the beautiful people, the positive people, the desirable people as friends. We are supposed to collect friends who enhance us. And, we should shun the other so-called negative people. I even heard one expert refer to these people unworthy of our friendship as 'toxic' people, people who will drag us down. Often, these are the people who really need friends. Of course it is probably much easier and customary to put up these discriminating criteria and all sorts of qualifications on friends. Do you qualify to be their friend and do they qualify to be yours?   I mention this to make it perfectly clear that these exclusions are completely opposite to goodwillie goals. When we say "*to all*" we mean "*to all*". Besides our way should be different from the norm. It is after all a revolution, a goodwill revolution.

To improve relationships with people we have got to upgrade our relationship skills, our people skills. To do that we need to examine them closely and see how and where we can improve them. How do we treat people now and how can we do better?

Friends

Rodney King posed the question, "*Why can't we all get along?*" Get along is not good enough. For goodwillies the question is the one raised by that rhythm and blues group called War which asks instead, "*Why can't we be friends? Why can't we be friends?*"

I am a goodwillie means I *want to be friends with everyone.* It fully recognizes that this is   a tall order if not virtually impossible to achieve. Besides people have all sorts of different criteria for friends. Regardless of what we do we may never qualify. We can only control our actions. So if we can't become friends with everyone, let us try to be friendly with everyone. As goodwillies we must make a constant conscious effort to avoid the actions which discourage friendship and do those that make us more likeable. So we need to first of all investigate what are the traits that make us likable and the ones that make us unlikeable?

Like - Why do you like someone? Because they are:
1. funny
2. friendly
3. same race as you
4. pretty
5. smart and intelligent
6. kind
7. unselfish

8 good listener
9.interesting
10.pays attention to me
11 shows concern for me
12 shows concern for others
13 upbeat
14 laughs at my jokes
15 hates the same things I do
16 likes the same things I do
17 brave
18 educated
19 considerate
20 understanding
21 witty
22 fun-loving
23 serious
24 ambitious
25 honest
26 tactful
27 other ----------

Dislike - Why do you dislike someone? Because they are:
1.loud
2. Rude
3. Obnoxious
4. Stupid
5. Insulting
6. Inconsiderate
7. Selfish
8 uneducated
9. domineering
10 bossy
11 boring
12 too talkative
13 no sense of humor
14 mean
15 boastful
16 lecherous

17 unpopular, unliked by others
18 rich
19 other race or religion, nationality
20 derisive
21 belligerent
22 uncaring
23 constantly puts people down
24 profane
25 withdrawn
26 cowardly
27 insincere
28 lies
29 dishonest
30 steals
31 low status
32 poor/rich
33 unpopular with others
34 too complaining
35 snobbish
36 insensitive
37 ugly
38 fat/thin
39 bad dresser
40 ignores me
41 too depressing
42 too religious
43 too argumentative
44 too embarrassing
45 too unfriendly
46 too negative
47 too nosy
48 other -------------
Rank the top 10 in each category.

"The unexamined life is not worth living" or how do you stack up on your own rankings? Hopefully this self-examination will point out areas you need to improve.

As a goodwillie we must always strive to do things to make people feel good. Making someone the brunt of jokes is very popular but it does not make that person feel good. Derision, sarcasm, and ridicule do not make the subject of such actions feel good. It does the opposite. So goodwillies must give up these. Too many have become so accustomed to using and accepting these traits as essential to making conversation interesting, that they might be reluctant to give them up in our "*Yo mama*" society. They feel compelled to display their acid wit by picking on someone for 'goodhearted' ribbing. It might seem trivial, but this 'goodhearted ribbing contributes to the acceptance of a certain meanness in our culture.   Remove some sort of derision from some people's conversation and they would be mute. As goodwillies we need to be on the lookout to avoid traits like these that make people feel bad. We might be very comfortable with them, even dependent on them, but they are not worth holding on to.

Be a friend to everyone
"A stranger is a friend that I have not yet met." - Unknown
"I never met a man I did not like." – Will Rodgers

"I do not want any friends". My friend of many years said that to me with great conviction. I was lucky to be the exception but unfortunately such a statement is not uncommon among many people. It is a symptom of how our society has deteriorated until friends have become undesirable. Through the goodwill revolution we seek to reverse that. Our money-centered culture has so devalued people that they are undesirable or unworthy of the effort as friends. We seek the comfort and refuge of money at the expense of friends. Besides, we fear our offer of friendship might expose us to the pain of rejection, the uncertainty of distrust, fear of insincerity and the risk of exploitation and vulnerability. Yes, so many withdraw to the security of money, of materialism and abandon fickle unreliable 'friends'.

So what is our society to become, a bunch of isolated money-seeking hermits? It seems headed that way but we goodwillies rebel against that trend. We do not go along with this devaluation of people. We revalue them. We consider people to be very important to our society. We, like the Quakers, seek a society of friends so we seek to befriend all. We unashamedly and without reservation seek goodwill towards all. This is the primary goal of the goodwill revolution. We want to befriend everyone. We must take the initiative to reach out as others are unlikely to do so.

This is not easy, especially in our jaded society. In this quest we will face distrust, insincerity, exploitation and even ridicule. We have got to use all our skills, good judgment, all of our smarts, to overcome these real obstacles in order to accomplish this. Yes, we can anticipate strong opposition especially from the victims of the money addiction, but we must fight on. But, this goodwill revolution is unique from other revolutions. Many other revolutions despite their outstanding merits, have had their reign of terror. But not the Goodwill Revolution. For goodwill is our goal and also our means. We will win over our opponents with goodwill. We will seek to make friends of them, to convert them to be goodwillies too.

Enemy and the role of retaliation

Enemies are friends with problems.

What is an enemy? Someone we dislike? Not good enough. Someone who does bad things to us or to our friends?

It happens all the time . An enemy has done you a great wrong. He might have insulted your mother. He might have ridiculed you. He might have told an evil lie about you. What do you do? Generally if someone does something mean to you then you want to retaliate by doing something even meaner to them. Retaliation means escalation. It's payback time. Even if a friend does something bad to you, you want to pay the friend back. But, let's take the worse case scenario. An enemy does something mean to you. Shouldn't we aim for the best most desirable outcome of that situation? The popular and acceptable response is to retaliate so severely that the enemy will not do it again.

But that is not the best possible outcome. The best possible is that your enemy becomes your friend. And, if that is the best outcome, should we not do what it takes to achieve it? Goodwillies always go for the best possible outcome first.

Would you rather people:
1. Like you
2. Admire you
3. Respect you
4. Fear you

5. Leave you alone

We, goodwillies, are not afraid to admit that we want people to like us. We think this is a very worthy goal and a goal which most people share, but secretly.

Do Good Deeds

I remember driving home from work one evening. I was about 2 miles from home in heavy traffic, when suddenly my clutch seemed to have gone haywire. I struggled to maneuver the car to the shoulder, where it finally came to rest and anger and frustration descended on me as I bemoaned my complete mechanical ignorance. Within seconds another car pulled over and out jumped a white youth.

"I saw you pull over. Problem?" he asked. I explained what happened and the next moment he was lying on the ground peering under my car.

"The clutch cable is broke. It's not too serious and the gas station across the way should be able to fix it." And he was gone with a "heigh-o silver!" "Who was that masked man?", I wondered. "To stop so spontaneously and help an old middle-aged black man that he did not know from Adam." The benevolence of the act overwhelmed my frustration and I felt good that sunmmer evening. Not only then, but when I think back about that kind spontaneous act, I feel good all over again.

A goodwillie strives to do good deeds. Good deeds makes you feel good. It makes the person you did the good deed for feel good also and even people who observe the good deed feel good too. In fact doing a good deed can be more satisfying than buying a Lexus. The novelty soon wears off, the payments become onerous, and it does not generate the good feelings in others particularly.

A popular antidote for feeling unhappy, which does not really work, is to go out and, yes, buy something impulsively. Lots of people swear by that remedy, but let me emphasize. *"It does not work!"* I wonder who ever came up with that idea. Probably some Madison Avenue advertising exec. *"Just go into debt and you will*

*feel better." "Buy something you do not need and you will feel
better."* Get real. If you really want to feel better, do a good deed.
Find someone to help. There is power in good deeds. They are
therapeutic.

GQ

We need to get in the habit of doing good deeds. We drive
every day so be on the lookout to be courteous and yield the right
of way to other drivers or pedestrians whenever we can. We spend
most of our waking hours at work, so seek ways to be friendly and
do good deeds to all your co-workers. The more we do them, the
more conditioned we become and the easier it will be.

So doing good deeds are an essential part of being a
goodwillie. When was the last time you did a good deed? I think
tangible goals are a good thing so maybe goodwillies should set
themselves a good deeds frequency target. How about at least one
good deed per month? In order to establish some sort of our own
personal measurement of our goodwillieness, we could use a sort
of GQ, a goodwillie quotient. This good deeds frequency would
then become a part of your GQ. So let us define GQ as the number
of good deeds per year, which would mean that a frequency of 1
per month would be equivalent to a GQ of 12. Aim high!

Do it anyway

We have stated that doing good basically is its own reward.
But, not always. Unfortunately, and much too often, we encounter
ingratitude, *"sharper than the serpent's tooth"*. Yes, ingratitude,
does hurt and can undermine your resolve to do good. Gratitude is
nice, but don't expect it nor even set it as a condition. Do it
anyway.

Fortunately a more comprehensive guide has already been
established for goodwillies to follow. It is the Paradoxical
Commandments by Dr. Kent M. Keith. Goodwillies, obey these
commandments. Nail them up on a wall and check yourself from
time to time.

The Paradoxical Commandments
   by Dr. Kent M. Keith

   1. People are illogical, unreasonable, and self-centered.
      Love them anyway.

2. If you do good, people will accuse you of selfish ulterior motives.
   Do good anyway.

3. If you are successful, you win false friends and true enemies.
   Succeed anyway.

4. The good you do today will be forgotten tomorrow.
   Do good anyway.

5. Honesty and frankness make you vulnerable.
   Be honest and frank anyway.

6. The biggest men and women with the biggest ideas can be shot down by the smallest men and women with the smallest minds.
   Think big anyway.

7. People favor underdogs but follow only top dogs.
   Fight for a few underdogs anyway.

8. What you spend years building may be des- troyed overnight.
   Build anyway.

9. People really need help but may attack you if you do help them.
   Help people anyway.

10. Give the world the best you have and you'll get kicked in the teeth.
    Give the world the best you have anyway.

Goodwill can make you invincible

Extending goodwill to strangers is actually easy. But, maintaining goodwill to someone close to you, who has betrayed you, has stabbed you in the back, is really tough. Overcoming treachery is probably the biggest hurdle and is probably why so many relationships between family and friends have been poisoned. Enduring loss of trust and bitterness can come from the slightest of misdeeds too and especially among families. Feuding is just not allowed. The healing of relationships is very important to goodwillies so be committed to using all your skills, patience and resolve to try to heal things. Good relationships are better than bad ones so why not work towards creating, maintaining and restoring good ones? It's hard. Your anger, your pride, your compulsion to retaliate, gets in the way. But, if you overcome these to maintain goodwill a bonus lies ahead. The more you do this the stronger you will get and after awhile you will become invincible. Those knives in your back will bounce back and will no longer hurt you.

In addition, there are many who will try to abuse and exploit the very good deeds that you do. But, goodwillies do it anyway. But let me emphasize once again, goodwillies are required to use all their skills and wits and intelligence to use good judgment in the performance of these good deeds.

Appreciation

Ever been to a sports event? The batter hits a home run or the soccer player scores a goal. The spectators erupt in tremendous applause. They show their appreciation. Appreciation is so important. It is so important that it should not be given only to athletes and rock stars and people of that ilk. Goodwillies should always strive to express their appreciation for good deeds. It is what the shrinks refer to as positive reinforcement. Good deeds make us feel good and by expressing appreciation we encourage the generation of more good deeds. Ok, so we don't have to jump up and cheer, but a simple compliment can do wonders. And, it is so easy to do.

Taking things for granted is the enemy of appreciation. Often we do not even take notice. We are probably so conditioned to that but we must resist it. To resist this we must pay attention to the triple A's.

1.   Be Aware
2.   Acknowledge
3.   Appreciate

Goodwillies should always be on the lookout for reasons and opportunities to compliment. I always go out of my way to compliment people as long as they deserve it. They don't have to perform Nobel-Peace-Prize-winning stuff too.

Diversify your friends

Do you have any black friends?
Do you have any white friends?
Do you have any Asian friends?
Do you have any Hispanic friends?

If the answer is no to any of the above, then get some. No excuses. Diversify your circle of friends. Seek them out. Use all your charm, ingenuity and skills to cultivate the friendships with these and any other ethnic groups. Of course not only ethnic groups but across religions and all those other traditional barriers. Do not be apologetic or timid about making friends. Remember, it is a goal to be proud of so go to it with purpose and enthusiasm.

Diversify your institutions

On a personal level, we have the power to pick our friends, so we have the power to diversify our friends. On the institutional level, however, we do not have such power.

As a black person and I am sure it is for almost every other black person, when I attend a social event, the first thing I do is check if there are any other black persons there. I see a play, a movie, a dance group, a band, a work place, any type of a meeting of an organization, a selection of government officials, etc., I immediately look for black representation. I am automatically sensitive to this. As goodwillies we have to develop this type of sensitivity to representation of not just our own but all ethnic groups in our desirable institutions.

The greatest obstacle to this diversity is negative stereotyping. As goodwillies we must be vigilant and fight against this to promote and be a catalyst for diversity.

Everyday Goodwillie

We have got to incorporate goodwillie traits in our everyday life so that it becomes a habit. We drive every day. Don't let other drivers cut you off. Beat them to the punch and yield the right of way to them. We go to a restaurant or the supermarket and encounter a surly server or clerk. Most people react by trying to out-surl them. Others avoid such persons, but, as a goodwillie, I seek out the surly person and try to make them cheerful. I do it all the time and my unexpected friendly reaction usually shocks the surliness out of them. I feel good and they feel good. Mission accomplished.

If a minority family moves into your neighborhood, reach out to them. Get to know them and make them feel welcome.

Most of your waking hours are spent at work. So the workplace is a good place to hone and practice your goodwillie skills. Be sure to befriend all co-workers but go even beyond that. Consider your co-workers and you a team and try to generate team spirit. Having played sports all my life, I think the camaraderie it engendered was even better than the sport itself. So, why not in the ordinarily dreary workplace too?

Goodwillie in the family

Money and materialism have taken their toll on the family too. Goodwillie like charity begins at home. In our contemporary society in which money has devalued people and relationships, it is inevitable that family relationships have been hit hard too. Family ties have given way to family feuds. The family which should be the foundation of our society is in pieces everywhere often the result of petty squabbling. The ties are not valued so at the first sign of friction, they break and very little attempts are made to re-establish them. Holding family members together takes work and effort, but these days too many do not value the family enough and are too pre-occupied with material things to do that. Our priorities are so high on material things, that family relationships like other relationships with people lose importance, suffer from neglect, and disintegrate.

Where did we go wrong? There was a time when blood was thicker than water and family ties were valued and strong. Now blood is thinner than water and family ties are insignificant and weak. Good strong family ties are very positive and rewarding. Goodwillies want to reverse that trend. Good strong family ties are extremely high priorities and we will strive to re-energize and maintain them.

Scenarios

- Father is dead. Eighty-year-old mother, who is not in good health herself, lives alone with occasional visits from children, who all live in big houses, easily capable of providing a comfortable home.
- Parents have done well and retired to their retirement mansion, while their son or daughter struggles on their own to raise a couple kids, mired in a low paying job. Forced to live in a run-down virtually unsafe area.
- Granny dumping - the practice of abandoning aged relatives at emergency rooms of hospitals because of the expensive medical care that they need.
- Son lives with and off mother in an abusive relationship.
- Aged parents are warehoused in nursing homes virtually abandoned by offsprings

Types of families – Nuclear and Extended

Once upon a time the family consisted of the mother, father, children, grandparents, uncles, aunts, nephews, nieces and even more members. Today this type of family hardly exists anymore other than in name only. This type of family is fast becoming a relic of the past and is now referred to as the extended family. This type of family has been whittled down to the bare nucleus to consist of just the mother, father and the children. Hence, the nuclear family is fast replacing the extended as the acceptable norm. Of course this nuclear family unit even gets smaller yet with DINKS. DINKS is the acronym for another even smaller family unit, the "Double Income No Kids" unit This consists of just husband and wife who elect not to have kids.

I suppose one rationale is the less people, the less complicated. But, our society is awash with family problems.

- Aging parents don't want to be a burden to their even successful kids.
- Grand parent living alone in comfortable home but lonely for too busy kids
- Social security grandparent with health problems struggling to make ends meet and battling high prescription costs

- Grown kids don't want to be a burden to their parents regardless of the harshness of their social and financial position
- Kids move out but hard times force them to move back and encounter embarrassment and social ostracism for so doing.
- Grandparents and aunts who used to play an important role in the upbringing of the children are relegated to curious spectators or mere bystanders.
- TV and comedians stereotype parents as dumb, irrational, and disagreeable which spills over into the society

What a great concept, marriage and the family. Ah those famous words of consolation. *"You are not losing a daughter, but you are gaining a son."* Marriage is supposed to join not only a man and wife but their families. It is intended to create out of two families one big extended family, in which some members are joined by blood and others are joined by law, the in-laws. What a wonderful concept. What a wonderful network for support such a union of families could be. If that new network is strong, it seems reasonable to assume that it will reinforce that marriage and make it stronger too. So in theory, marriages have the potential to create all these networks of people and thus strengthen the ties in the whole society. So much for theory. Marriage, which should bring families together, in fact, often drives them apart.

One spouse's beloved mother is perceived as an unwelcome interfering busybody by the other spouse

One spouse sees the other spouse's family as inferior and unworthy

Even more problematic is the other type of family, the "blended family". This is the family in which either husband or wife or both bring kids from a previous marriage. It has its own unique problems added to the mix like deserved or undeserved "evil stepmother" stereotype, unfair treatment of one spouse's kids, and dealings with the often hated 'ex', to name a few.

In summary, we need to be a friend to everyone and that includes family members. Being a friend to everyone is not easy. It is quite a challenge. So how do we show that we want to be friends with everyone. We do this by being considerate, polite, understanding, friendly, compassionate, kind, caring to everyone. One of the greatest satisfactions is overcoming a challenge and the greater the challenge, the greater the satisfaction. If someone says that it is difficult to do or worse yet, it is impossible to do and you actually do it, there is a great feeling of satisfaction. Being a goodwillie is not easy and it is a day to day challenge, so there is a great feeling of satisfaction in just being one. Many goodwillie goals are tough to achieve, but they set the direction and are important compass points along the way to improvement. Improving relationships is just such a goal.

Chapter 9
Better Than Dick Cheney

The quality of our leadership.
The quality of our political leaders is almost irrelevant. How can we expect to have good leaders when good does not count? Our leaders don't have to be good. They don't have to be fair, generous, compassionate, just, understanding, considerate. They do not have to have a record of doing good deeds. They do not even have to be very intelligent.

Is Dick Cheney good? Is it important? Should it be important? We are helpless to do much about this and at this rate, even worse than Cheney is likely to follow.

In 2001 Dick Cheney became the Vice President of the United States. How could almost half of voting America support such a man for the second most powerful position in the US, maybe the world?

Easy. Because he is:

- Rich
- Powerful
- Has strong corporate support especially from powerful oil companies
- able to hire top advertising companies to make him a saleable product, regardless of his past

But does he deserve to be the leader of men? How does he stack up? I remember as kids we would often challenge each other with the taunt, *"You think you better than me?"*

Is Bush/Cheney better than me?
Is Bush/Cheney morally superior to me?
Kinder than me
Fairer than me
More considerate than me
More compassionate than me
Is he more concerned about the plight of the starving people in the developing world and elsewhere than me

Is he more concerned about the injustices especially towards blacks and others than me

Is he friendlier, more respectful to all people than me

Yes, I am better than Bush/Cheney because I am morally superior, because I am a goodwillie. In all honesty I consider myself better than Dick Cheney, the Vice President of the United States of America (and his boss too for that matter). Dick Cheney is richer than me. Dick Cheney is more powerful, has more prestige, than me. But, I am better than he. It is easy to be better than a man who I repeat:

• was one of only two US Congress members who voted against a resolution calling for the release of Nelson Mandela from prison

• voted against the Equal Rights Amendment which stated " Equality of rights under the law shall not be denied or abridged by the United States or any state on account of sex."

• repeatedly opposed economic sanctions on apartheid South Africa in 1985, 1986 and 1988.

The fact is any goodwillie is better than Dick Cheney. For what does 'better" really mean. We forget that 'better' is the comparative for good. Logically, if English were logical, it would be "gooder". Therefore to be better you don't have to have sacks of money, bristling with power. These things are irrelevant. But you have to be good. You have to do good deeds, be kind, compassionate and possess similar virtues. So in our competitive society, we goodwillies will compete to be truly "gooder" to be morally superior not just for our own benefit but for the society also.

Even the scum of society, by joining the Goodwill Revolution, can be better than Dick Cheney.

I Wanted to Live
or Drive-by Shooting

I wanted to live
I wanted to run and jump
To laugh, to play

To dance, to sing
Even to cry some more
I wanted to live
Some more
More than six
Six short years
I wanted to live

Up three floors
Behind locked, bolted
And barricaded doors
On that lime green chair
With the gray shiny tape
On one tattered arm
But on which I liked to play
It searched me out
It found me there
I no longer will play
On that broken chair
I wanted to live
But your bullet found me there
I wanted to live
More than six
Six short years
I wanted to live

I wanted to live
I wanted to grow some more
I wanted to go to junior high
To senior high
Be a cheerleader
"Hey! Hey! Wha'do'ya say
Turn that ball the other way!"
My graduation ceremony
My mother so proud of me
I wanted to live

I wanted to live
I wanted to love

To know the feeling
That first kiss
The exhilaration
To hunger for that special touch
Of that special one
And give myself to him
To wed
My little daughter
Just like me
But to work to make her
Better than me
I wanted to live

I wanted to live
I wanted to hold
My grandchildren in my lap
And tell them stories
Like my grandma
Used to do
And indulge them
Give them candies
Spoil them
Teach them to say
"Hello"
"How do you do?"
About the five little piggies
Who went to market.
Like my grandma
Used to do
I wanted to live
For more than six
Six short years
I wanted to live
I wanted to live

And how about you?
Do you feel remorse?
Or am I just another notch
On your gun?

Another boast to your buddies?
An uneventful incident?
Nothing?
Was it an armed robbery?
Or a drug bust gone awry?
Or did you miss the head
Of some disrespectful friend?
And found 6-year old me
Instead?
Or was it just frivolity?
Could it have been
Deliberately?
Or just shooting
Your beloved gun
Indiscriminately?
But,
I wanted to live

I wanted to live
And the outrage of my death dies down
And my killer they tell me
Was abused from infancy
The system's to blame
Not he
It's because it stole his dignity
He was just trying to be a man
I should forgive
I should understand
But, I can not
Probably because
I wanted to live
I wanted to live
I wanted to live
And also because
I am dead

Conversation With A Gang Leader

So you killed that poor little girl. You were poor. The poor
have the worst of everything. All the avenues to riches are pretty

much blocked. They receive the worst education, the worst educational environment. They have insecure dead-end low-paying jobs. They have the worst housing, healthcare, and entire living conditions in general. Being poor by definition is not having enough money to get all these things. It seems like and is a hard way to live. *Now you are a cold-bloodied killer.*

And you were the worst kind of poor, black ghetto poor. If people in general are devalued for material things, then the poor are considered completely worthless. The American poor by international standards live in luxury. They have TV's, refrigerators, running hot and cold water. But, that same TV blares at them day in, day out,

"Unless you have a Lexus, you are nobody."

"Unless you wear designer basketball shoes, you are nobody."

His woman must designer-dress to impress or he will be a nobody to her. So the self-esteem of the poor gets tied up in these expensive material symbols and they do not have the means to acquire them. Besides:

- Radio talk shows tell them they are just a drain on society.
- Their ghettoes are racked with crime and drugs.
- They receive very inadequate police protection although they need more than any other group.
- Their kids grow up in fear and under constant danger of becoming victims of or enmeshed in the drug and gang culture.
- More and more they are a political liability as the cause of the poor diminishes.

The only thing worst than being poor is to be black and poor. Most ghetto poor are black.

You were poor and unwanted. But your gang wanted and accepted you. It made you feel nice to belong. You did their bidding and earned their respect. So you robbed, you mugged, you sold drugs, you terrorized the community and even killed four people and this innocent girl.

But now you are not poor. You have lots of money to buy lots of things. You have money and power. The American dream. You are feared but not respected. You are hated, despised and loathed by your own community. You have become someone that not even a mother could love. Does your girlfriend really love you or just likes the nice things she gets from you? How could anyone love someone who has killed an innocent 6-year-old girl? Can you even love yourself? You are a fugitive from the law. Any day you may be killed by the police, a rival gang member, or a trusted member of your own gang. You killed an innocent 6-yesr-old girl. People consider you the scum of the earth.

Dick Cheney is a gang leader too. His gang killed many innocent 6-year-old Iraqi girls with their war against Iraq. And they did not kill just four other people but they killed thousands of innocent Iraqi people. Dick Cheney and his gang already had lots of money and power even before they did these dastardly deeds. But, you are pond scum and Dick Cheney is revered.

But, there is good news. You can be better than Dick Cheney. Join the Goodwill Revolution. Repudiate this money madness, all that addiction to materialism and the phony happiness it promises. Become a goodwillie. Break your enslavement to money that has lead you to become a monster. Instead of evil, selfish, terrorizing deeds, do good deeds for your community. Are you ashamed to do good deeds? Are you afraid to do good deeds? You are brave enough to kill innocent people but are you brave enough to do good deeds? You are a leader. Your gang members recognize this. So be a leader for good. Be a leader of a goodwillie gang. Instead of terrorizing your neighborhood, protect it and shower it with goodwill. Instead of loathing and hatred, earn the respect and admiration of your community.

You can make that ghetto bloom. Work to transform that hostile ghetto into a friendly community where people care about each other. Work to make it a place where 6-year-old girls can play safely without fear. Work to make it a place of hope instead of a place of despair. You know firsthand about crime so work to make it a crime free environment.

You cannot bring that innocent 6-year old back to life. But you can dedicate your life to making other 6-year old girls have better lives by becoming a goodwillie. As Bob Marley asks,"Are you satisfied with the life you're living?" To choose to remain on your present course is to choose to remain despised, loathed, and unloved. Choose to be a proud goodwillie instead. To choose to be a goodwillie is to choose to be better than Dick Cheney.

And, your first job as a goodwillie is to call up your rival gangleader and ask" How can we be friends? How can we make our community better for all?"

Moral Superiority

Goodwillies aim to be better than everyone else. This is not an arrogant statement. This is because to be better than anyone else, one has to be morally superior. In our competitive society, we goodwillies compete to be morally superior because that competitiveness will produce a better world. For to be morally superior you have to be kinder, fairer, more just, more compassionate, more honest, and so on. Morally superior persons don't kill, don't pollute the atmosphere to make an extra buck, don't exploit and victimize workers, don't drop 2-ton bombs in a residential neighborhood in Iraq, and so on.

In our society today, money and power rule and dominate. But this is a revolution, a goodwill revolution. Money and power will define esteem no more. The better person is the morally superior person. And it is really democratic. Money and power is irrelevant. It does not matter if you are rich or poor, black or white, Christian or Muslim, or all those other categories people find themselves, you have equal opportunity to be morally superior. So I don't care how much money you have Bill Gates, you are not better than I. Your obnoxious, repressive, unfair, unjust boss at work is a nobody for all his power over you. Why? Because he is obviously very morally inferior. In reality he is a pitiful figure running amok. So thank God you are not cursed with his obvious character flaws. *"There but for the grace of God go I"*.

So with such a perspective, moral superiority can give you the power to endure. It is fortifying. I think it is what Shakespeare meant when Brutus said in Julius Caesar, *"There is no terror, Cassius, in your threats, for I am so well armed in honesty, that they pass me by, like the idle wind , that I respect not."*

So Bush, Cheney, and the repressive boss at work, all become *"like the idle wind which I respect not"*. I wish I could help them.

Chapter 10
Goodwillie To The Rescue of Religion

Don't blame it on Jesus or Allah

Religion has the reputation throughout history as being one of, if not the major causes of wars. And the great contradiction is that all these religions embody a high standard of ethical and moral principles. But, despite this, they have precipitated the most bloody and devastating and of course un-ethical and immoral wars.

Too often religion which is supposed to embrace peace and love has brought instead war and hatred. Unfortunately, that is true even today and is becoming worse. A religious fundamentalism is sweeping the world with its by-product of intolerance, hostility and even wars. The Middle East is a prime example. But even here in U.S.A., just watch some TV evangelist arouse auditorium-packed throngs by promising that for some poor unfortunate souls that they dislike "God will burn them in hellfire!" Such a mass display of passionate hatred is frightening.

Even within these religions, there is vicious fighting. Shiites versus Sunnis, Catholics versus Protestants, fundamental type TV evangelists battle every other religion, Christian or otherwise. Too many think they've got the only true god and the other religions are inferior. Some are considered so inferior that their followers don't deserve equal treatment unless they convert, if they even have that option. Of course, we know that unbelievers have been put to death.

Religion in fact does not deserve this horrible blame. Let's not blame it on Jesus or Allah. The fault lies in a religious fervor or hysteria that is too easily whipped up to burn so-called heretics. This religious fervor is the real villain which distorts and suborns true religions, breeds hatred, distrust and injustice and is among the worst scourges that mankind faces today.

Not long ago, this religious fervor was not restricted to religion. It was bad enough there. But no, it attached itself to economic systems. Yes, communism and capitalism. These were the new religions and the world reeled from their inquisitions, their holy wars.

The USA was the superpower that championed the religion of capitalism. The other superpower, the Soviet Union championed the religion of communism. Both superpowers claimed great idealistic goals - freedom, justice, prosperity etc. but instead they plunged many a poor country into a life of terror and devastation. These superpowers victimized these poor countries in order to keep them true believers. The primary victims of this religious fervor were essentially third world countries. This anti-communist religious hysteria was exploited very well there in Nicaragua. Our mercenaries there, the so called contras, hired by our taxpayer money and trained by our CIA manual, were used by us to deliberately murder innocent doctors, teachers, farmers etc., and to commit other clear acts of terrorism aimed at undermining the social structure there. How hypocritical we must seem to be when we deplore terrorism elsewhere. There was a time that the American public would not tolerate this but would be filled with shame and outrage. Nowadays, blind support for such shameful policy of gunboat diplomacy, military intervention and intimidation, terrorism, invasion and even war, is considered one's patriotic duty.

But this religious-like hysteria was not limited to this type of action. It was also used to whip up support for the stockpiling and development of more and more destructive, virtually suicidal weapons, which threatened the entire planet with extinction.

This religious hysteria even turns one against ones own people, against ones own friends, against one's own family. The inquisitions of the Red Guard and McCarthyism are examples. Such phrases as "creeping socialism" produced a knee jerk reaction of horror. To simply accuse, mind you, only accuse, someone of being a communist or even having "communist leanings" was to depict that person as being a little worse than a child molester. Since this religious fervor is capable of stirring such passions, such blind passions, a shrewd cunning person or persons may use it as tool to exploit the masses. History is full of just such persons and even today many have recently sprung up into full bloom.

If such communist allegations could turn us against friends that we have known, loved and respected, you can imagine the effect such allegations had on strangers. They did not have a chance. Worse yet if these strangers are foreigners and weak and relatively defenseless as Nicaragua.

When we look back historically at these religious and pseudo-religious wars, they seem so ridiculous. How could those people have been so stupid, so hypocritical, so contradictory, and so blind? Was even the conquering Joshua of Jericho fame such a hero? What was Jericho's crime for it to have its entire population killed? It is clear when we look back that man has been blinded by this religious hysteria in the past. But, do we have to wait for history to be objective? With a world chock full of nuclear arm, can we afford to wait on the objectivity of history? I say no. We have got to discard this religious hysteria now and adhere to the true ideals such as justice, love, fairness, and compassion and dedicate ourselves, to those. There is hope. There is the Goodwill Revolution.

The Goodwill Revolution to the rescue of religion

The goodwill revolution strips religion of the venom attached to it. It extracts the best qualities common to all religions and leaves the dogma behind. We will shy away from their doctrines but we will embrace the aspects of all their doctrines that unite us and support the goodwillie principles. The goodwill revolution acknowledges these different religions only for the sake of deliberately reaching out and extending goodwill to people with different religions from us. Religion will separate us no more.

The goodwill revolution itself is derived from the message of Christmas. "Peace on earth. Goodwill towards all men". Goodwill towards all mankind is universal to all religions and is the primary goal of the goodwill revolution. These days the true message of Christmas is lost in a buying frenzy. Christmas should be a big peace festival, a special time to promote goodwill towards all men instead of the awful commercialisation it now represents. So, this is not just a Christmas message, but it is the inspiration for goodwillies and the Goodwill Revolution. If we want peace on earth, we have to have goodwill towards all men. Just as the Christmas message has been distorted to buy, buy, buy to excess, so also has our lives been distorted to buy, buy, buy to excess. And as religious as we claim to be, our true god becomes "money", money to buy, buy, buy to excess.

Despite what your preacher says, the Bible is clear and consistent on this point. *"You cannot serve God and mammon."* (Luke Chapter 16 v 13) Mammon is money, wealth, riches. When a rich man came to Jesus Christ and asked what should he do to achieve eternal life. We goodwillies are not as extremist as Christ, when He told the rich man to sell all that he had, give the proceeds to the poor and follow Him. When the man refused, Christ said *"It is easier for a camel to pass through the eye of a needle, than for a rich man to enter into the kingdom of God."* (Luke Chapter 18 v 25)

Christ threw the money lenders out of the temple. But, guess what? They're back. The church and big money are intertwined. Fundamentalist churches like the Moral Majority are economic empires themselves.

The bible is relentless in attacking the pursuit of money as a goal. However, this message is strangely absent from our contemporary rich religious leaders. We goodwillies clearly have the bible on our side on this issue.

In the Bible, Paul raises the question of what is the greatest virtue? He then went on to reduce it to three finalists. In justifying his selection of his top choice, Paul produced some of the most quoted and most beautiful verses in the Bible. When I was younger, the translation identified the three as faith, hope and charity. The contemporary translation now has changed charity to love. There is a big difference between charity and love. Charity denotes a sense of giving to the poor, a sharing of ones fortunes with the less fortunate. The dictionary also defines it as an act or feeling of benevolence, goodwill or affection.

Love is even harder to define. There are all sorts of love, romantic love, puppy love, maternal love, kinky love. Love uplifts, hurts, ennobles. As a popular Jamaican song asks *"If love's so good, how come it feels so bad?"* Everyone seems to have a different understanding of what love is and is the basis of many types of action, some good, some bad. Love is different things to different people.

For these reasons I think the translators could have come up with a more definitive word. The meaning of goodwill is unmistakable so I think this is much more appropriate. So with my revision substituting *goodwill* the 1 Corinthians selected verses from Chapter 13: (King James version)

"1 *Though I speak with the tongues of men and of angels; and have not* **goodwill**, *I am become as sounding brass and tinkling cymbal.*

2 And though I have the gift of prophecy, and understand all mysteries, and all knowledge; and though I have all faith, so that I could remove mountains; and have not **goodwill**, *I am nothing.*

3 And though I bestow all my gifts to the poor, and though I give my body to be burned, it profiteth me nothing.

....

11 When I was a child, I spake as a child, I thought as a child: but when I become a man, I put away childish things.

12 For now we see through a glass, darkly; but then face to face I know in part; but then I shall know even as I am known.

13 And now abideth faith, hope and **goodwill**, *these three, but the greatest of these is* **goodwill**."

Chapter 11
Goodwill as Foreign Policy

War is not the answer nor peace
If we have an enemy, what do we do about it?
1. Fight him – but risk severe consequences
2. he might beat you up and do you severe injury.
3. A fight could escalate to weaponry resulting in death and incarceration.

4. Abuse him verbally
5. Build alliances against him – get friends to dislike him
6. Discredit him to others
7. Ignore him

As a person or a country, we react pretty much the same. We fortify ourselves against the enemy.

As a country, it is considered the best possible strategy to make sure we are stronger militarily. This is pretty much the universal reaction. This is definitely the Pentagon reaction. So we get bigger and more guns, bombs and all the weapons of war to defend ourselves against this enemy. When the enemy was the Soviet Union, it did likewise, creating an arms race. This arms race has dominated our society and has been very effective in producing weapons of mass destruction, probably far exceeding our wildest expectations.

But arms are not enough. We also try to get our friends involved to form alliances with us and against our enemy.

Nothing stirs the blood more than calls to defend against the enemy. The Pentagon has used this to bloat the military budget year after year even though with the demise of the Soviet Union, America is the only superpower. The rationale for this policy is that this is the best defense for if you are stronger than the enemy he will not attack you and if he does you will make mincemeat of him. Even at peace, arms build-up continues. There is animosity. There is tension. There is insecurity. This type of policy is typical all over the world and is passionately adhered to as the best way to deal with an enemy.

The world is wrong! There is a better way to deal with an enemy. We should try for the best possible outcome. Too often the present policy results in the worst possible outcome, war, with all its death, terror and destruction. In Iraq, we have achieved the worst possible outcome, with its death and destruction, even worse than we ever expected. Even peace is not a good enough outcome. The best possible outcome is for enemies to become friends. That should be our personal goal and our foreign policy goal. You name it. The way to achieve that goal is through goodwill towards all.

BPO – Best Possible Outcome

In the words of the late reggae singer, Peter Tosh, "*I don't want no peace. I want equal rights and justice.*" Well for goodwillies, peace as a foreign policy is nice, but it is not enough. We don't want to just tread water, we want to move. We want goodwill to other countries to be our foreign policy. We want a policy that will seek friendly relations with every country. We want a policy that transforms countries that are our enemies into friends.

Right now not even peace to all countries is our foreign policy. The buzz words that describe our policy is "*to pursue American interests*". How selfish! In the relentless pursuit of these interests, more and more, we have used our status as the one and only superpower to become the international bully of the world. We have invaded more countries than any other country. In January of 2003 when we were poised to attack Iraq. King George II, a.k.a. George W. Bush, branded Iraq and North Korea as two members of the "axis of evil.". But when Time magazine conducted a poll in which they asked of the three countries, the US, North Korea and Iraq, which is the greatest threat to world peace? Of the more than 130,000 Europeans that responded, North Korea received about 9%, Iraq 13% and the winner, the US with a whopping 78%.

And almost every country we have attacked has been weak and powerless and pretty much incapable of defending itself against us. In addition in pursuit of "American interests" we have overthrown governments, destabilized economies, undermined leaders, blockaded harbours and let's not forget the 40 year-old economic embargo of that poor tiny country of Cuba . At the behest of multinational corporations, we have decimated the banana trade of Caribbean countries, countries who thought America was their friend, and now face economic catastrophe.

Many other countries are misled into believing America is their friend. The reality is that they are considered friends only if they serve American interests. The leaders of Saudi Arabia are now our friends. Check them out in about ten years. Those leaders will probably end up like a couple of former friends, Noriega of Panama and Donald Rumsfield's former friend, Saddam Hussein.

There is nothing friendly about America's foreign policy. It's tools are fear, threats and intimidation. The goal seems to be submission. No one likes a bully and not even our propaganda can make us likeable to others. We are the leaders of the world and the rest of the world too is following a goal of serving their own 'self-interest'. It it any wonder then that
we live in a dangerously polarized world that seems to get worse everyday.

- Catholics vs protestants in Northern Ireland
- Brutal tribal and civil wars in Liberia, Sierra Leone, Ivory Coast and many other countries of Africa
- Genocidal murder of millions in Rwanda
- The horrors of ethnic cleansing in which rape was used as a weapon in former Yugoslavia
- The Tamils vs Buddhists in Sri Lanka

In these countries peace is not enough. Peace has proved elusive. Peace should only be a stage on the way to creating goodwill. Let the goal not be just world peace but world goodwill. Let us seek to convert enemies into friends. America is the world leader and has to lead not by words but by deeds. Right now we do neither but are perceived as the most belligerent nation in the world and the greatest threat to world peace. The fact is that we have the power to make cultural change throughout the world and are doing it. But let's not limit that change to fostering belligerence and eating Big Macs. Instead let us adopt a goodwillie policy, a policy of goodwill to every nation. Let us seek goodwill, support goodwill, nurture goodwill, promote goodwill. Let us be friends to all countries and as friends we will have more beneficial influence in achieving desirable goals. By adopting and promoting a foreign policy of goodwill to all countries, I am sure we will bring not just world peace but world goodwill closer to a reality.

Conflict Resolution – Goodwillie Style

The greatest problem in the world today, ranging from individuals to mighty nations, is conflict. If we could effectively resolve conflicts the world would be a much better place. Most conflicts go unresolved and for good reason. We are going about it wrong. Generally resolution involves some give and take between adversaries and some compromise is worked out. Give and take means one side loses a little and the other wins a little. In retrospect, one side might believe they gave too much and the other might believe they gained too little. Detractors usually believe one of these and could lead to a simmering discontent or breakdown of the agreement. So often these resolutions are fragile things, especially when dealing with emotionally charged issues like international, racial, tribal, political and religious differences.

The goodwillie way is completely different. It requires us to be guided by goodwillie principles of creating goodwill to all. In almost every conflict, each side believes right is on their side from their perspective. They perceive that they are doing something good for their cause. Not always. In some instances, one side is intent on doing bad. This is called exploitation and such is more difficult to resolve even the goodwillie way. Isn't it ironic that both sides are intent on doing good, but such evil can come from these conflicts such as murder, violence, and wars. The goodwillie way is different because it taps into those good intents, which is completely ignored in other methods. This is the real key to successful resolution. What is the cornerstone of the Goodwill Revolution? Goodwill to all. So the first step in solving the conflict is for the adversaries, regardless of the issue, to agree upon the goal of seeking goodwill between each other and the parties they represent. The goal is not peace, but goodwill, friendship. *"How can we be friends?"*

Countries embroiled in border disputes and other type of festering hostility, sometimes based on some major or trivial reason like tradition, need to negotiate on how create goodwill. Extend the hand of friendship, and make that the primary goal.

Our goal is to resolve this conflict as friends not as adversaries. As friends, the original issue becomes a shared problem between friends and stands a better chance of resolution to the satisfaction of both. It becomes a joint problem and is seen more objectively from both perspectives.

But is it feasible?

I don't know for sure, but we have to try. We will lose nothing by it and we have so much to gain. It is a difficult task and for it to have any chance of success, we must put people with skills, experience and commitment to these ideals in charge.

But we must also recognize that there are warlords. They have power and prestige. If there is no war, they lose this power and prestige. For these warlords, power and prestige are invested in the continuation of discord and hostility. Can we see a Donald Rumsfield, a Dick Cheney handling such a policy? Only if we want it to fail. Too often peace negotiators are some bellicose bloodthirsty blowhards more intent on out-intimidating each other rather than finding real solutions. Instead, we need to learn from the examples of others, others who have transformed enraged violent hostile warring communities, some polarized by race, ethnicity, and religion, from enemies into friends. People like these are often undervalued but they are the real leaders and are valuable assets.

In the midst of the most vicious violence and brutal killing and reprisals, Amram Mitzna, Mayor of Haifa has succeeded in creating a different reality of tolerance, mutual respect between different parts of the population, between Arabs and Jews, and between secular and religious. Haifa is the home to 250,000 residents, members of five different religions, living together in harmony, peace and respect.   Asked about his successful leadership in Haifa, Mitzna said that "today, the "Haifa Model" has become a brand name. My hope is that I will succeed in leading the State of Israel in the same reality that exists in Haifa." "This type of coexistence has made Haifa a role model for other cities in Israel and throughout the world." Unfortunately, as I mentioned time and time again, such people are undervalued and Amram Mitzna was no exception. The Israelis did not choose him to lead the State of Israel. They chose the warlord Sharon instead.

Farrakhan reconciles with Jews

A momentous event took place in Kingston Jamaica in April 2002. Most people do not know of it. Louis Farrakhan, the controversial leader of the Nation of Islam not only reconciled publicly with the Jews in Jamaica but was a special guest in the synagogue there in Kingston. They even allowed him to address the congregation in the synagogue there and he did. In that address he said:

".....we felt that the leadership of Jamaica should applaud openly what you(Jamaican Jewish leaders) have done, so that when the word goes forth to the United States and to Europe and to wherever Jews may be on this earth, that they will say they took a bold step, now let's take one in the United States as well, because if we can mend and heal the wounds between our two communities, I can say that there is a possibility that we will be able to heal the wounds in Palestine and in Israel today. It is my hope and my prayer that yes, from this place, from this holy place, a new beginning can emerge".

The word did not go forth. It was a moment of international significance but the American and world press was silent. Congratulations to the Jewish leadership in Jamaica. They have showed up the hypocrisy and fraud of the rest of the world and this has been a crowning achievement for which Jamaica should be proud.

The fact is that Minister Farrakhan *(whose father was Jamaican)* has held out the olive branch to Jews in America before and they have rejected him. Most conspicuously was at the time of the Million Man March on October 16 1996. He made every effort then to reach out to the Jewish establishment then. They shunned him and the American media again acted as if it never even happened.

The best possible outcome in the deep rift between Farrakhan and the American Jewish leaders is that they become friends. He is now friends with Jews in Jamaica. What a wonderful thing it would be for the Nation of Islam and American Jews to reconcile and even become friends? Are the American Jewish leaders seeking that? Are they seeking reconciliation? It seems obvious that American Jewish leaders, the American media and the American establishment do not want this reconciliation.

The media did not want it nor did they want people to know of Farrakhan's attempts to seek it. It did not fit into their plans to continue to demonize him. Do we really need more evidence how the media manipulates and distorts the news? They are not to be trusted.

Surely minister Farrakhan has said some very vile things about the Jews. But, he has said some equally vile or worse things about Jesse Jackson. But, for the Million Man March, Jesse and he stood together in reconciliation as brothers and have remained so. So also could have been the case with American Jews. Isn't this what religion is all about, reconciliation, redemption, bringing adversaries together, the lion lying down with the lamb? Can you imagine the impact if the American Jews had done then, what the Jamaican Jews have done in Jamaica? Are you really surprised it did not happen here in America? Not in America!

The American Jewish leaders knew very well if they had accepted Farrakhan's invitation to meet to try to heal the differences between their communities, they would have faced severe ostracism. Do you know from whom this very severe ostracism would come? From 'good' respected people again. These 'good' respected people Jewish and non-Jewish are obstacles to healing! If I were not a goodwillie they would make me sick! Is there any wonder why there are such difficult problems in the world today? Is there any wonder why large numbers of people here in America support that malicious illegal war and occupation in Iraq?   Is there any wonder that in the 2004 presidential elections here in the US, lots of people said, "Give us Barrabas?"

We have got to recognize and change the corrosive environment here in America that clings to hatred and adversity and really seek goodwill towards all instead. Friendly relations between Farrakhan and American Jews are possible and should be a goal of Jewish leaders. They have rejected him times before, so now they should be brave enough to seize the initiative and reach out to him and ask, "How can we be friends?"

The healing of Crown Heights
In 1991 in the Brooklyn section of Crown Heights, a 7-year-old boy, Gavin Cato, whose family was from Guyana, was struck by a

car driven by a member of the entourage of the Lubavitcher Grand
Rebbe Menachem Schneerson, a very orthodox Jewish sect. The
child died.

Three hours after Gavin was struck, Yankel Rosenbaum, a
29-year-old Hasidic scholar from Australia, was fatally stabbed by
a mob. For two more days and nights, rioting followed. It was
Jews against blacks, which include a large number of West Indian
immigrants.

However, by January 2003, relations jn Crown Heights had
become so good that, the Community Council president, a Jewish
woman, was nominated by a black woman. The previous president
was a black woman.

"*The goodwill of people is causing all of this,*" the incoming
president said. "*People want to live in peace. They want to have
good relations. They want to be good neighbors.*" Her election was
just one more sign of the community's ever-increasing spirit of
cooperation between blacks and Jews.

"*Crown Heights is a very exciting community,*" said New York
Police Department Brooklyn South Commander. Rabbi Jacob
Goldstein, president of Community Board 9 since 1980, added,
"*People are working together and sitting together.*"

In the words of Crown Heights City Councilman James Davis :
"*Crown Heights is a community of African-Americans, Caribbean-
Americans, Jewish-Americans, Latino-Americans and Asian-
Americans all living in harmony. ... We are a shining example of
what dialogue and communication can accomplish.*"

Leaders credit former Borough President Howard Golden,
other elected officials, community board chairmen and district
leaders and the police for their work immediately after the riots to
restore calm.

There were also groups such as Mothers to Mothers, founded
by Henna White, a Lubavitcher, and Jean Griffith Sandiford, an
African-American whose son, Michael, was fatally struck by a car
while running from a mob of whites in Howard Beach. The two
women worked together to establish talks among women - talks
that continue to this day.

The Crown Heights Community Mediation Center was set up
and Project CARE was organized for networking among
community groups. Organizations such as the United Coalition of

Block Associations address basic neighborhood concerns, such as where traffic lights are most needed.

Medgar Evers College, established in Crown Heights in 1970, played a major role in preparing young people for leadership. Jewish leaders hail the school's president, Edison Jackson, for his efforts to make the college a place where all are welcome.

The 103-year-old Brooklyn Children's Museum provided programming for children of the community.

The Jewish Children's Museum, a $23 million project on Eastern Parkway was constructed. This museum is not just for Jews but is a museum for all children, a place where they can come and get a taste of what Jewish history and culture are all about.

The precinct council also plans lots of activities for black and Jewish children. In addition to an annual family picnic, there is an end-of the-year party and skating parties.

Lesson

Surely there is a valuable lesson to be learned here for the many troubled spots all over the world. The Crown heights experience should serve as a model for the warring conflict-ridden world. It is a tribute to the ability of goodwill to bring harmony, mutual respect and friendly relations among different and hostile peoples. In Crown Heights, real leaders from all walks of life emerged. They used goodwill, not just to create peace but to create goodwill to all, to create friendly relations. Those are the type of leadership we need so desperately among leaders of our mighty nation and nations all over the world.

Two rights make a wrong.

We have often heard it said that *"Two wrongs do not make a right"*. However, one of the main causes of international conflict is that *two rights make a wrong*, and a horrible wrong too. In international conflicts, typically both sides think they are right and these two 'rights' have often led to horrendous consequences.

The Israel-Palestine conflict is a perfect example. The Israeli leaders want to do good for their people. The Palestine leaders want to do good for their people.

Both sides want to do good and think they are right, but we are witnessing the alarming consequences.

The goodwillie way is for the Israeli leaders to want to do good for all the people and the Palestinian leaders to want to do good for all the people also. There is only one right, doing good for all the people, both Israeli and Palestinian! If the goal is not goodwill to all, we will always have conflict.

So in the Arab-Israeli conflict, attempts to seek peace are pretty much doomed to fail. The only chance for success is to seek goodwill and appeal to the goodness of all sides including extremists, as long as all sides agree to seek goodwill to all. It worked in a similar seemingly impossible situation in apartheid South Africa. So quoting once again the words of Nobel Peace Prize winning Nelson Mandela,

"Historical enemies succeeded in negotiating a peaceful transition from apartheid to democracy because we were prepared to accept the inherent goodness in the other."

In my little elementary school in Jamaica, the Lottie MacMillan Sunshine School, mottos were very popular sources of inspiration to learn. One popular one was , *"What man has done, man can do"*. So, yes, Virginia, world goodwill is feasible. But it will take work, marshalling all the forces of goodwill and capable of creating goodwill, skills, vision, determination and commitment to make it happen. We need godwillie political leaders, goodwillie colleges, professors, goodwillie press, goodwillie corporations, goodwillie religious organizations, all sorts of goodwillie institutions. We probably don't need them all but the more the better. Help make it happen yourself. Become a goodwillie now and start the process rolling.

Chapter 12
Corporations – The Good, the Bad and the Ugly

Nowhere does the evil prosper and the good perish more than among corporations. This is because our system rewards the bad corporations and punishes the good ones. This is a clear formula for disaster and in time good corporations will disappear completely.

Corporations exist to make money. If they provide a better service, they will make more money. If they provide a better product, they will make more money. Or if they do better product and service, but for less, they will make more money. Competition between corporations will produce better and better for us consumers and everyone will be happy. The good old profit motive will thus provide us with better products and service. That's the way it was supposed to work but something has gone horribly wrong.

Money is the problem. The problem is corporations exist to make money. If money is the goal and money is a corrupting influence, it is bound to corrupt corporations. It has. It has created large powerful ruthless, disreputable corporations. These corporations are plundering America, decimating our working man, stealing our democracy and eliminating competition with good reputable corporations. Just as the seven lean kine ate up the seven fat kine in Joseph's dream in the Bible, the bad corporations are eating up good corporations voraciously.

Employees are not people
These big greedy disreputable corporations manifest the most widespread devaluation of people. To these corporations employees are not people but just overhead. The duty of corporations is to cut overhead in order to maximize profits. So corporations will ruthlessly cut staff, depress wages, and reduce health care benefits regardless of the devastating effects on their employees.

And if that is not enough, they will ship the jobs overseas via globalization where they may be performed at slave wages rates and where environmental and other sweat shop abuses may prevail. Of course the greedy corporations are not the only one who benefit. A lot of people do. Vast numbers of people do. These people are called consumers. Low wage product means cheaper prices. Consumers are delighted to get cheaper prices. The corporations sell more. The consumers buy more from them. The corporations make more money and the consumers save more money. The consumers are pretty much ignorant of the real cost in exploitation of the employees and former employees but in all probability to most of these consumers, it would not matter. Consumers have been conditioned to ignore those abuses. Those victimized employees don't count. The more money we save, the more money in our pockets. More money in our pockets makes it all right. Of course we are all consumers. So we all have a vested interest in the devaluation of people for the sake of money.

The good reputable corporations on the other hand keep these jobs here in America, observe fair labour and environmental practices. They keep Americans working on good-paying jobs. They allow their members to join unions. Yes, Virginia there are good corporations who do not sacrifice their employees for the sake of the almighty dollar such as:

Malden Mills and Aaron Feuenstein epitomize the good corporation. On December 11, 1995 a fire burned most of Malden Mills to the ground and put 3,000 people out of work. The little cities of Lawrence and Methuen in Massachusetts were in deep gloom as they thought it was the end of their jobs and their communities. But in these times where corporations like AT&T are laying of thousands to boost stock prices, Aaron Feurenstein, the owner of Malden Mills, did the unthinkable. Aaron Feuerstein spent millions to *keep all 3,000 employees on the payroll with full benefits for 3 months.* To him those 3000 people were more important than millions of dollars of his own money as he explained "'The fundamental difference is that I consider our workers an asset, not an expense.. 'I have a responsibility to the worker, both blue-collar and white-collar,' 'I have an equal responsibility to the community. It would have been unconscionable to put 3,000 people on the streets and deliver a death blow to the cities of Lawrence and Methuen.

And this is not the first time too that Mr. Feurenstein displayed such sterling goodwillie qualities. In 1981 his textile mill went bankrupt. He did not pack up his mill and move to some cheap-labour country overseas like so many other corporations. Instead Aaron Feurenstein spent millions to develop a new product and re-opened the mill *in Massachusetts* with all the highly paid unionized workers (high-paid by global standards). His firm created Polartec® and Polarfleece®, revolutionary new products. As a result jobs were saved and he came out of the bankruptcy stronger than he went in.

Aaron Feurenstein was the CEO and owner of Malden Mills. If on the other hand, Malden Mills were a publicly traded company, the shareholders would never have allowed his heroic rescue to take place. The destiny of the towns and their workers would have been very low priorities to the shareholders. Such considerations typically do not belong in the corporate world. The shareholders would be only interested in making money so they would have fired him and the towns and its workers be damned.

But can you run a business the Aaron Feurenstein way? According to Mr. Feurenstein *"'Before the fire, that plant produced 130,000 yards a week.. 'A few weeks after the fire, it was up to 230,000 yards. Our people became very creative. They were willing to work 25 hours a day.'"*

How about for a publicly traded company? In this current corporate environment good deeds are punished or at least are considered incompatible. But Ben and Jerry have chosen the high road and have proven that a good socially conscious corporation can prosper.

Ben and Jerry's – model of a goodwillie corporation

Ben and Jerry's Homemade Inc. epitomizes a goodwillie corporation. Like any other publicly traded corporation, it seeks sustainable and profitable growth and to increase its share value for its stakeholders. But, beyond that Ben and Jerry's is unlike most other companies. The high values that they practice defy the corrosive money-grubbing policies of the typical big corporation and is a miracle that they can not only survive but also flourish under these conditions.

We know all about Bill Gates, Donald Trump, Sam Walton, but how many ever heard of Ben Cohen and Jerry Greenfield?

This is a duo who really deserve to be household names. In 1978, these two founded their ice cream, yogurt and sorbet company in a renovated gas station in Burlington, Vermont with a $12,000 investment of which $4,000 was borrowed. Today its markets include the US, Canada, Mexico, Europe and Korea. Besides it franchises or owns over 230 Ben &Jerry's ice cream shops ('scoop shops').

In 2000 the Unilever corporation bought Ben and Jerry's for $171 million. Nevertheless, this Ben and Jerry subsidiary still maintains its unique socially conscious method of operation relatively independently of its new owners so far. In two years under these new owners little has changed the impressive Ben And Jerry's social mission much to the relief of Ben and Jerry's supporters who feared that role would have ended.

Its goal is not just profits. Instead it seems profits are only secondary to its self described progressive , nonpartisan social mission that seeks to meet human needs and eliminate injustices in our local, national and international communities. They do this by integrating these concerns into their day-to-day business activities. Their focus is on children and families, the environment and sustainable agriculture on family farms.

So, unique it is, but hopefully it will become the new standard for corporations. Some of the highlights of its operations are:

Minimizing waste to help preserve the environment.

Pursue policies designed to help to bridge the widening gap between rich and poor inevitable in capitalism.

Support sustainable and safe methods of food production that reduce environmental degradation, maintain the productivity of the land over time, and support the economic viability of family farms and rural communities.

Support for and cooperation with unions. The employee handbook is so worker friendly that it was used as a model for the contract negotiated with the union

Established a policy of a liveable wage. They defined a liveable wage as the starting salary for a single person that will sustain a quality of life that includes expenditures for housing, utilities, out-of-pocket health care, transportation, nutrition, recreation, savings, taxes and miscellaneous expenses. In 2000 this amount was calculated to be $9.40 per hour not including benefits. Compare this with the federal minimum wage of a mere $5.15 per hour in 2004.

Also in 2000 the ratio of the highest paid Ben and Jerry's employee to the lowest was 17-1. Compare that with current trends. According to *Business Week's* annual survey, the average CEO of a major corporation made $12.4 million in 1999, up 17 percent from the previous year. That's 475 times more than an average blue-collar worker and six times the average CEO paycheck in 1990. A study on the CEO-worker pay gap by the Institute for Policy Studies and United for a Fair Economy reports that if the minimum wage, which stood at $3.80 an hour in 1990, had grown at the same rate as CEO pay over the decade, it would now be $25.50 an hour, rather than the current $5.15 an hour.

Five per cent of pre-tax profits are shared by all employees annually.

It offers its employees a very good health insurance plan in which Ben & Jerry's bear 80% of the premium and at times have absorbed as much as 1 million dollars in additional expenses caused by rising premiums.

Partnering with non-profit organizations to set up Ben And Jerry's ice cream shops. These scoop shops are independently owned and operated by community-based nonprofit organizations. Ben & Jerry's waives the standard franchise fees and provides additional support to help nonprofits operate strong businesses. These shops offer supportive employment, job and entrepreneurial training to youth and young adults that may face barriers to employment.

Employee Diversity as it strives to make a conscious effort to maintain a diverse workforce.

Franchise Ownership Diversity is a direct goal even though complicated by the traditional barriers to minority ownership. At the end of 2003, 81% of our shops were independently operated and 24.6% (57) of those operators were women or people of color.

Supplier Diversity - policy designed to evolve the program towards certified minority and women-owned businesses and socially aligned suppliers such as:

St. Albans Cooperative Creamery - As a farmer member-owned business, this supplier represents an alternative economic model. the Co-op a premium of $480,000 to provide milk from cows that they have pledged have not been treated with rBGH, a genetically engineered growth hormone use to increase milk production.

The Greyston Bakery of Yonkers, New York, a supplier of brownies to Ben & Jerry's since 1988, is owned by the Greyston Foundation, a nonprofit social service network that operates its bakery to train low-income people for self-sufficiency. Some of these people have been without homes for some time.

Aztec Harvests - A cooperative in Oxaca, Mexico which provides fair trade coffee extract. Cooperative members use organic agricultural methods.

Philanthropy - Ben & Jerry's gives over $1.1 million dollars annually to the philanthropic Ben and Jerry's Foundation. The Foundation is managed by a nine member employee board which makes grants primarily to organizations committed to social and economic justice, community activism and sustainability.

We have got to change that corrosive money-grubbing corporate culture. We have got to change that corporate culture so that Aaron Feurensteins and the Ben and Jerry's will flourish. We have got to change that culture to create goodwillie shareholders who will support and encourage the Aaron Feurenstein CEO's. We have got to change that culture so that goodwillie values prevail in the corporate boardrooms.

The products of goodwillie corporations are bound to be more expensive. The American consumer will buy the less expensive product. Good patriotic American consumers will abandon these companies to save money. That will be the reward of good corporations for protecting American jobs. These companies will either go bankrupt, or will have to exploit their employees, or even worst, must ship their good jobs overseas too, in order to survive.

This was not always the case. We once could protect our workers from such unfair competition from underpaid foreign workers by imposing a tariff on these unfair imported products. We had control. But powerful corporations changed that. The American public paid little attention to trade policy. But the big corporations did and beyond. They focused on it and dominated it so that they were able to change it for their benefit and at the expense of American jobs.

Wall Street anti-worker tactic

Of course Wall Street runs America and is the sacred temple of the money pushers. So, it is not surprising that one of the most devastating blows against the American working person has come from Wall Street. Mergers abound. One corporate raiding tactic was for the corporate raiding corporation to buy out another corporation and to promptly cut operational expenses. Translation : cut hundreds of employees. Cut staff and company stock price goes up. No wonder there has been a frenzy of job layoffs by numerous corporations. So the corporate raider makes a bundle and people lose their jobs. Meanwhile the remaining employees are forced to do twice the amount of work and are also so grateful to still have a job. Once again this puts in motion the vicious circle. Reputable corporations are soon forced to do likewise or perish.

The press is no friend of the working man. The working man does not own or spend sizeable sums of money to advertise in the press. But, these big greedy corporations do. So instead of deploring these callous policies, the media actually praises them. The popular way of doing this is to declare that the company was overstaffed and bloated and that laying off the workers was a good shrewd business move.

So with the media spewing this propaganda, job deprivation has becomes acceptable to the public. But not only for corporations, this job cutting mania is especially popular now to the largest employer of people in America, the government. It is even easier for the public to swallow since government employees are already stereotyped as lazy and deserving to being laid-off anyhow. The more government staff is cut, the less effective government will become, The less effective government becomes, the less effective they will be able to monitor, regulate, and enforce, the compliance of big, ruthless, corporations. At this rate, government will soon become just a toothless impoverished lapdog easily run over by these big powerful money-pusher corporations.

So with the media and most politicians in the hip pocket of, or intimidated by, those 'bad' powerful corporations, the only advocate supporter of the rights of the working man left, is the union. These bad corporations recognize this and so are intent on eradicating this sole obstacle to their complete undermining of the rights of the working man. Although most workers have the legal right to form unions, nearly all employers launch ruthless anti-union campaigns, using both legal and illegal tactics to thwart workers' right to choose a voice on the job. According to the AFL-CIO:

Fully 92 percent of employers force workers to attend meetings where bosses argue against the union. Employers can legally force workers to attend these meetings. Workers who refuse to go can be fired—legally.

More than three-quarters of employers force workers to sit in one-on-one meetings with their supervisors to "change their minds" on unions.

One-quarter of employers illegally fire workers involved in union activity.

Today's labor laws allow employers to "predict" (although not "threaten") that a workplace will shut down if workers vote for the union, often scaring and intimidating workers out of exercising their freedom to choose a union.

Our nation's labor laws are enforced so feebly employers routinely get away with breaking them.

When employers are punished, the penalties are too weak to deter other unscrupulous employers from breaking the law.

Fully 32 million workers in the United States—including independent contractors, first-line supervisors, some government workers and agricultural workers—have no right to collectively bargain under the law at all, according to a September 2002 report from the General Accounting Office.

This type of thing indicates how tough a fight the unions are in. Companies hire, at great expense, specialists in the art of union-busting. Weak laws, anti-union corporate media, and the proliferation of union busting experts, have succeeding in driving down the number of union members in the US.

Fair trade chocolate and coffee

Of course the abuse of workers by these big multi-national corporations is not limited to the confines of the USA. At least, here, workers have some protection, but especially in developing countries, these corporations can virtually do as they like. So, as expected, worker abuse is lots worse.

But some of the worst abuse of workers by bad corporations take place abroad. These big powerful corporations take advantage of the desperate conditions in third world countries to amass huge profits. Oil is the largest commodity imported by the US. Number two is anther type of fuel that gets so many started in the morning. It is coffee. We consume one-fifth of all the world's coffee, making us the largest consumer in the world. But few Americans realize that agriculture workers in the coffee industry often toil in what can be described as "sweatshops in the fields." Many small coffee farmers receive prices for their coffee that are less than the costs of production, forcing them into a cycle of poverty and debt. And things are getting worse, as in the last decade, the major coffee companies' revenues have doubled while the earnings of ordinary coffee farmers have been slashed by two-thirds. Millions of coffee farmers around the world who depend on their harvests to provide for their families are facing debt and starvation

But for that sweet delicious chocolate that you love so much it is probably even worse for those who work on the farms. "Sweatshops" would be an improvement for many of them as in Cote d'Ivoire (Ivory Coast) the world's largest chocolate grower and some other African countries, slaves work the farms. And not just slaves, but child slaves, who are abducted to work the coca plantations that produce chocolate. Even with slave labor, the price farmers receive from these big powerful multinational companies is so low that they themselves barely stay above the poverty level.

The days of 33 cents per gallon at the gas pump are long gone. Just as gasoline receives a fair price, coffee and chocolate deserve the same. There is a movement to achieve such a fair price for these products, a movement which goodwillies should enthusiastically be a part of. It is called the Fair Trade movement. Companies become Fair Trade certified by paying a predetermined minimum   price   for   these   raw   products.   Conscientious organizations such as Global Exchange, Transfair and OXFAM has conducted an uphill fight to promote Fair Trade certification, but the big companies have resisted, as they continue to churn out big profits.

Fair Trade coffee has become a growing segment of the $55 billion coffee industry although the coffee makes up only about 2 percent of the global supply. The big four coffee companies pretty much control the markets. They are

1. Proctor and Gamble, producers of Folger
2. Sara Lee Corp., the maker of the Hills Bros. and Chock Full o' Nuts brands
3. Kraft Foods unit of Philip Morris Companies (Altria), the maker of Maxwell House
4. Nestle producer of Nescafe

According to OXFAM, these companies pay the farmer 24 cents per pound and sell it for $3.60 per pound. The fair trade price is currently $1.25 per pound.

While the global price for cocoa hovers around 40 cents per pound, the Fair Trade system guarantees farmers 80 cents per pound.

Check Global Exchange, OXFAM, and TransFair USA for more of the gory details as these three organizations are leading the fight to promote Free Trade certified products.

Vote with our dollars

Politicians are helpless. Even if they mean well and do not actually receive money from these disreputable corporations, they are afraid they could be targets for removal by them. So politicians, even well meaning ones, are intimidated into helplessness. But we goodwillies are not helpless. We can vote these bad corporations out. Let's vote them out. Let's vote them out with our dollars and every day is election day. We are not gonna put our dollars into their cash register ballot boxes. Every goodwillie must make a personal commitment to refrain from continuing to buy from and patronize these disreputable companies. Goodwilles must support good reputable corporations

The goodwillie aim is not to destroy but to rehabilitate these bad corporations, to make goodwillie corporations of them. We have the power to do it.

Chapter 13
Martin Luther King's Murder and the Goodwill Revolution

Doctor Martin Luther King was brutally assassinated on the balcony of the Lorraine Motel in Memphis, Tennessee in 1966. He was felled by a single shot from a rifle. They killed the dreamer. They have almost killed the dream.

But why was he killed? That is the key. Do you know who killed him? Many readers think it was James Earl Wray. And why not? He confessed to the crime and served many years in prison for it. Even I, who pride myself on my knowledge of such things, up to recently was under that false impression. James Earl Wray did not kill Doctor Martin Luther King. It is not theory. It is public record, but strangely seems to be an obscure fact. It is an obscure fact because we depend on the media for 'facts' and the media downplayed and buried that story. We have become too dependent on the mass media for 'facts' and validation which bestows on them gigantic power to distort and mislead. They do so now with great relish and do not deserve our trust

James Earl Wray was a decoy in the conspiracy which killed Dr. King. This is no wild-eyed conspiracy theory although there are many who would like to brand it so. Once again, this is public record. The King family in time became suspicious of the many incongruities in the James Earl Wray conviction. There evidence was so compelling that they convinced then US Attorney General Janet Reno to re-open the case. They also launched a civil suit into the wrongful death of Dr. King. A trial was held. It was no 'OJ' trial of the century as it strangely received virtually no media coverage. When it was over, a jury consisting of 6 whites and six blacks, came up with the verdict that Doctor Martin Luther King was murdered by Lloyd Jowers and 'government conspirators'. (For an excellent summary of the trial, read "The Martin Luther King Conspiracy Exposed in Memphis by Jim Douglass for Probe Magazine of Spring 2000. The entire report is also available on the web at: http://www.ratical.com/ratville/JFK/MLKconExp.html

But why was Dr. King killed and why then? One popular theory is that he was killed by a vengeful racist. Timing does not seem right for that. There were much better opportunities to kill him before when racial tensions were really at a fever pitch. His major civil rights accomplishments had been achieved. He had already won the Nobel Peace prize and his popularity had already crested. Besides he had lost some support and was berated by the media for coming out against the Viet Nam war. Many people were wondering why should a man of his stature be bothering with championing the cause of the lowly striking sanitation workers of Memphis. So why should a vengeful racist go to all that trouble to set up so sophisticated a plot to kill him then?

There is a lot of merit to the notion that he was killed to remove a popular black leader. But, once again it seems to me *'the time is out of joint'*. Such forces had the means to kill him earlier, before he achieved so much. Still it is a reasonable theory.

Another popular theory is he was killed because he had come out against the Vietnam war shortly before his death. Here timing, the proximity to his death and his harsh criticism of the war depicting the US as *'the greatest purveyor of death'* in the history of the world, makes this theory plausible. But for me doubts linger. There were many other prominent critics of the war, so why him?

Of course, a combination of all these reasons seemed very likely, which is probably the one I favored until …….

It was a Martin Luther King holiday. I had hit a rough patch in writing my book. I was struggling to pull it together. I was listening to Martin Luther King speeches on Pacifica Radio as I do every Martin Luther King holiday. I had heard these speeches before but I never tire of hearing them. Suddenly it hit me! Dr. King was not killed for what he did, but for what he was about to do! It was the last speech he gave . He delivered it right there in Memphis, Tennessee that April 3, 1968 on the eve of his assassination. How about that for timing? It was an apocalyptic speech titled "I have been to the Mountain Top".

In that final speech he uttered words which are key to our liberation from the domination of the ruling class and big rich corporations. These words form a vital aspect of the goodwill revolution. These are dangerous words even today. These are words which seemed inconspicuous at the time to most, but raised alarms and fury in the minds of certain powerful people and goaded them into deadly action. These are the words that sealed his fate:

"And so, as a result of this, we are asking you tonight, to go out and tell your neighbors not to buy Coca-Cola in Memphis. Go by and tell them not to buy Sealtest milk. Tell them not to buy--what is the other bread?--Wonder Bread. And what is the other bread company, Jesse? Tell them not to buy Hart's bread. As Jesse Jackson has said, up to now, only the garbage men have been feeling pain; now we must kind of redistribute the pain. We are choosing these companies because they haven't been fair in their hiring policies; and we are choosing them because they can begin the process of saying, they are going to support the needs and the rights of these men who are on strike. And then they can move on downtown and tell Mayor Loeb to do what is right.

But not only that, we've got to strengthen black institutions. I call upon you to take you money out of the banks downtown and deposit you money in Tri-State Bank-- we want a "bank-in" movement in Memphis. So go by the savings and loan association. I'm not asking you something that we don't do ourselves at SCLC. Judge Hooks and others will tell you that we have an account here in the savings and loan association from the Southern Christian Leadership Conference. We're just telling you to follow what we're doing. Put your money there. You have six or seven black insurance companies in Memphis. Take out your insurance there. We want to have an "insurance-in."

Now there are some practical things we can do. We begin the process of building a greater economic base. And at the same time, we are putting pressure where it really hurts. I ask you to follow through here. "

Doctor Martin Luther King was raising the prospect of a national boycott of 'bad' corporations! Many boycotts have been ineffective but he had the charisma, the reputation, the admiration and the experience to make it work. This is where he first came to fame, 'the Montgomery Alabama Bus Boycott! They could not take that chance. They had to nip it in the bud. He had to die.

An integral part of the goodwill revolution is the boycott of 'bad' corporations, not to drive them into bankruptcy but to convert them to good. As I said before, they have stolen our democracy, but now we goodwillies will vote with our dollars and every day is election day. And we are not just gonna boycott these bad corporations, we are gonna 'Montgomery-Alabama-Bus-boycott' them!

Alabama Bus Boycott

In 1955 Alabama municipal law forbade black people to ride in the front of the city buses. On December 1, 1955, Mrs. Rosa Parks, a forty-two year old seamstress, boarded a city bus and sat in the first row of seats in the black section of the bus. When some white men got on the bus, the driver ordered her to give up her seat and go to the back of the bus. She was arrested when she refused. Black leaders in the community including the Reverend Dr. Martin Luther King was enraged, met and set in motion plans to boycott the city buses.

- 40,000 hand bills were printed and handed out to members of the black community
- black ministers made calls for the boycott from the pulpits
- the boycott went into effect Dec, 5 1955
- it was immediately successful with 90% of black bus riders staying away and seeking alternate transportation
- that first evening the Montgomery Improvement Association (MIA) was formed with the Reverend Martin Luther King elected president
- on the 4th day of the boycott the MIA submitted a moderate desegregation plan similar to one already in operation in Baton Rouge, but city and bus officials rejected it
- city officials also forbade black cab services from charging less than 45 cent minimum fare, thus preventing them from continuing to charge the 10 cent fare they had been charging which was the same as the bus fare
- since the 45 cent fare was unaffordable to most blacks they faced a serious transportation crisis
- the MIA countered with an elaborate "private taxi" plan under which blacks who owned cars transported blacks who needed rides to and from designated points.

- Since very few blacks could afford to own cars, churches bought station wagons, designated as 'rolling churches' and provided invaluable service as private taxis
- The whites responded by canceling liability insurance four times in four months, but Dr. King ended up acquiring insurance from Lloyds of London
- When that did not work, police harassment of the drivers was used by arresting drivers for minor traffic offences. Dr. King himself was arrested at a pick-up point for doing 30 mph in a 25 mph zone.
- The white power structure tried to divide the black community. In one attempt they persuaded three non-MIA black ministers to accept a fake compromise and then publish this as MIA acceptance. Before it was published, MIA officials traversed the community warning of the hoax so that confusion was prevented and the boycott continued
- Whites then turned to violence, bombing the homes of Dr. King's and another MIA official E.D. Nixon.
- Whites the turned to the law arresting DR. King under an old antiquated law that prohibited boycotts
- Dr. King was ordered to pay $500 dollars plus $500 in court costs or spend 386 days in jail
- The boycott began to take a toll on white merchants in the city since the reduction of black travel meant reduction of black buying in the city. So these merchants formed their own group to negotiate an end to the boycott.
- The boycott was so effective that blacks scrapped the original weak bus desegregation plan for full integration one.
- On November 13, 1956 the US Supreme Court upheld a previous federal court ruling declaring segregation on buses unconstitutional, marking a victorious end of the boycott.

Chapter 14
Montgomery-Alabama-Bus-Boycott Them

Today we are faced with political helplessness because of the influence of corporate money which threatens our democracy. But, the Montgomery Alabama bus boycott is a model and an inspiration which shows that we have much more power than we realize. If blacks could prevail over all those obstacles such as:

- virtually no transportation alternative in place
- the laws, police harassment
- their poverty
- violence against them
- lack of any political representation if they even had the right to vote
- an established and widely accepted tradition of segregation
- hostility from the rest of the society
- divide and rule attempts
- jail

Then we can prevail over corporations too.

We can make capitalism work for us. In Montgomery, blacks had no alternative transportation system, but for every product we decide to boycott, there is another on the market.

We do not need fear police harassment, jail, violence or any legal prohibition from buying any product. The fact of the matter is that compared to the Montgomery Alabama Bus Boycott, the Goodwill Revolution boycott of the goods and services of 'bad' corporations is a piece of cake.

We Have Power

Martin had to die because he was about to reveal that we have power and was about to use it. And that power is buying power, but we have not really used it.

As consumers we are called upon to rescue the country from recession by spending our money. Consumer spending goes down, we end up in recession. Consumer spending goes up, we get out. Now that is awesome power to be able to control this country by our buying power.

Black spending

The University of Georgia's Selig Center for Economic Growth recently released "The Multicultural Economy 2003," in which black buying power is estimated to be around $688 billion. This represents tremendous growth. Even when it was $490 billion annually, it surpassed the Gross National Products of Canada, Spain, India and Mexico. These figures demand serious attention. This has the potential of real economic muscle. Dr. King was just beginning to advise blacks to flex that muscle back then by re-directing their spending away from companies that supported segregation. Many black advocates today are urging blacks to flex that muscle by redirecting their spending to re-invest in black business to uplift the black condition in America.

Black America has that much economic muscle despite their lower income levels. The goodwill revolution has the potential of generating even more power by redirecting their spending to patronize 'good' corporations only.

Integrity Buying and Social Investing

What are the criteria we use in buying? We have been looking for good quality at the lowest prices. Bargain shopping. For goodwillies these criteria are not good enough and will no longer be deciding factors. It is not a bargain if it is produced by:

- Exploitation of the worker
- The callous degradation of the environment
- Child and slave labor anywhere in the world
- Wages insufficient to live on
- Companies that Practice discrimination in the workplace
- Companies that force workers to work under unsafe and hazardous conditions
- Produced by union busting companies

Employer War Against Workers

Although most workers have the legal right to form unions, nearly all employers launch ruthless anti-union campaigns, using both legal and illegal tactics to thwart workers' right to choose a voice on the job. Most people are completely unaware of the vicious war that so many companies are conducting to intimidate and rob workers of their rights. According to AFL-CIO statistics:

- *Fully 92 percent of employers force workers to attend meetings where bosses argue against the union. Employers can legally force workers to attend these meetings. Workers who refuse to go can be fired—legally.*

- *More than three-quarters of employers force workers to sit in one-on-one meetings with their supervisors to "change their minds" on unions.*

- *One-quarter of employers illegally fire workers involved in union activity.*

- *Today's labor laws allow employers to "predict" (although not "threaten") that a workplace will shut down if workers vote for the union, often scaring and intimidating workers out of exercising their freedom to choose a union.*

- *Our nation's labor laws are enforced so feebly employers routinely get away with breaking them.*

- *When employers are punished, the penalties are too weak to deter other unscrupulous employers from breaking the law.*

- *Fully 32 million workers in the United States—including independent contractors, first-line supervisors, some government workers and agricultural workers—have no right to collectively bargain under the law at all, according to a September 2002 report from the US General Accounting Office.*

There was a time when we could depend on government to outlaw these practices, but not anymore. There was a time when we could depend on the media to expose and deplore these practices, but not anymore. It is up to us as goodwillies. We will have to practice integrity buying or positive patronage by boycotting the bad and patronizing the good.

Boycott Iraqi war supporters

But there is also an even greater reason than these to boycott companies. Goodwillies cannot   just be a witness to the abomination of the Iraq war and occupation. If we really believe in goodwill to all we must oppose it also with every moral fiber in our body. It is the moral equivalent of slavery, apartheid, the holocaust. Over 100,000 Iraqi's have been killed in a war based on lies. Two-thousand-pound bombs have been dropped on residential neighborhoods. We have used torture and human degradation. Water supply systems have been deliberately and systematically destroyed forcing the people to drink dirty and unsanitary water.

Goodwillies must oppose such a travesty, such crimes against humanity and in such a way that it counts. Goodwillies joined the record number of millions who participated in protest marches all over the world against that illegal war. But, all our protests were in vain. But, how could this happen? Good people let us down again.

I remember that Easter morn, the war was in full swing with bombs raining down on Bagdad like a video game. I was in church that Easter morn. "*He has risen!*" and the lusty singing of hymns could not keep the haunting specter of death and destruction in Iraq out of my mind. It was the midst of the war and support for the war was highest. According to the polls, 73% of these good Christian worshippers supported the death and destruction of innocent people who had never lifted a finger against the US. Good people have been manipulated again. Good people have failed us again as they failed us in slavery, in the holocaust, in apartheid and so many times in history.

Protest marches by millions failed. Letters to the editor failed. Letters to Congress and the senate failed. Now, even democracy failed when the warmonger was re-elected. It is time for the something new. The goodwillie way is not by voting power but by buying power, the mobilization of a boycott. The Goodwillie message is "*If you support those who support the war, then we wont support you.*"

George Bush, the Republican President, launched that illegal war so we shall select prime supporters of the Republican Party for boycott. Of course many Democrats supported the war also. Democratic presidential nominee John Kerry supported the war. Boycotting supporters of both parties would be ineffective. Instead we need to pit one party against the other by supporting the lesser of the two evils.

Every Republican leader supported the war, but at least some Democrats did not. Democratic Senator Robert Byrd of West Virginia fought many a lonely battle on the Senate floor against it. Two of the Democratic presidential contenders, Dennis Kucinich and Howard Dean spoke up bravely against the war. Democrats did not oppose it enough but clearly are the lesser of two evils. Clearly, the Republican Party is the war-mongering party. So we must boycott financial supporters of this war-mongering Republican Party.

The leader and proponent of this war based on lies, now insults our intelligence by justifying this horrible abomination by claiming that the world is better off without Saddam Hussein. Are the more than 100,000 Iraqis who have been killed by the war better off? Are the more than 1,000 American troops who have been killed better off? Is the 70% of the Iraqi workforce that is unemployed better off? I think not. But Halliburton and all the other war profiteering companies are better off! That's who. So we must boycott the financial supporters of this war-mongering Republican Party.

Old list misleading

List of top supporters of the war-mongering Republican Party (1999-2003)

    1 Altria (formerly Philip Morris) $6.5m

    2 AT&T $5.36m

    3 Microsoft Corp. $5.12m

    4 United Parcel Services $4.48m

    5 MBNA $4.38m

    6 Citigroup $3.93m

    7 Pfizer $3.9m

    8 FedEx Corp. $3.4m

    9 Bristol-Myers Squibb $3.4m

    10 GlaxoSmithKline $3m

    11 Wal-Mart $2.85m

12 General Electric $2.58m
13 ExxonMobil $2.35m
14 AOL Time Warner $2.31m
15 Anheuser Busch $2.23m
16 ChevronTexaco $2.2m
17 PepsiCo $1.9m
18 Schering Plough $1.8m
19 Archer Daniels Midland $1.8m
20 Wyeth (formerly American Home Products)$1.74m
21 Alticor Inc. $1.7m
22 American Airlines $1.62m
23 Ford $1.52m
24 BP Amoco $1.25m
25 Disney $1.25m

Even now in January 2005, many anti-war groups and others use this list as the basis of their boycott activity. There is one gigantic problem with this. The list is outdated and is no longer accurate. This leads to the penalizing of companies that have changed and no longer deserve to be there. For a boycott to be effective and meaningful, it must respond to positive change in a timely manner.

Here again we should practice the triple A's. Be A-ware, A-cknowledge and A-ppreciate. We should monitor these companies so that we become aware of desirable changes. If desirable changes occur, we should acknowledge these changes and express our appreciation to the companies. If we continue to boycott a company which has seen the folly of its ways and changed its policies accordingly, we are defeating our purpose if we do not react to that change.

Opensecrets.org is a great source of the latest on political contributions. They derive their figures from legally required financial disclosure statements. Based on figures from their website, I have compiled a series of tables and graphs to depict a more up to date picture of financial contributors.

The list is not complete as in some cases I was unable to locate 2004 data for some of the top donors from 1999 to 2003, such as Bristol-Myers Squibb, GlaxoSmith Kline, Schering Plough, Anheuser Busch, Archer Daniels Midland, and Wyeth (formerly American Home Products). Most donors give to both Republican and Democratic Parties, so it is very important to see the per cent of the total donation which was given to the Republican Party. This is called hedging your bet. In this way as mentioned before, both parties become dependent on financial support, although one party more than the other.

The first table compares top contributors to the Republicans on the old list of 1999 to 2003 with the 2004 presidential election year list.

The next table looks at some top Republican financial supporters of 2004. Donors who gave approximately 50% or more to the Democratic Party are not included, even though the actual amount given to the Republicans might be considerable.

Fast food and buying gas are such a regular part of our daily routine that they are products that so many people can boycott. Two graphs follow showing the top Republican supporters in these fields.

Top Supporters of the Republican Party (1999-2003) vs 2004						
*1999-2003		2004				
Company	Rep -mil	Total	Dem	Rep	Dem	Rep
1 Altria (Philip Morris)	$6.5	$912,927	35%	65%	$319,524	$593,403
2 AT&T $5.36m	$5.4	$644,069	48%	52%	$309,153	$334,916
3 Microsoft Corp.	$5.1	$2,911,939	61%	39%	$1,776,283	$1,135,656
4 United Parcel Servic	$4.5	$2,149,922	27%	73%	$580,479	$1,569,443
5 MBNA	$4.4	$1,328,322	24%	74%	$318,797	$982,958
6 Citigroup	$3.9	$2,317,897	53%	47%	$1,228,485	$1,089,412
7 Pfizer	$3.9	$1,402,127	33%	67%	$462,702	$939,425
8 FedEx Corp.	$3.4	$1,316,571	32%	68%	$421,303	$895,268
9 Bristol-Myers Squibb	$3.4	n/a				
10 GlaxoSmithKline	$3.0	n/a				
11 Wal-Mart	$2.9	$2,008,101	19%	81%	$381,539	$1,626,562
12 General Electric	$2.6	$1,651,262	46%	54%	$759,581	$891,681
13 ExxonMobil	$2.4	$550,717	12%	88%	$66,086	$484,631
14 AOL Time Warner	$2.3					
Time Warner		$2,588,802	80%	20%	$2,071,042	$517,760
15 Anheuser Busch	$2.2	n/a				
16 ChevronTexaco	$2.2	$390,081	17%	83%	$66,314	$323,767
17 PepsiCo	$1.9	$262,199	34%	66%	$89,148	$173,051
18 Schering Plough	$1.8	n/a				
19 Archer Dan. Mid.	$1.8	n/a				
20 Wyeth	$1.7					
21 Alticor Inc. $1.7m	$1.7					
Alticor/Amway		$238,788	0	100%	$0	$238,788
22 American Airlines	$1.6	$521,964	36%	64%	$187,907	$334,057
American Air/AMR 2002		$1,221,203	44%	55%	$537,329	$671,662
23 Ford	$1.5	$729,084	28%	72%	$204,144	$524,940
24 BP Amoco	$1.3	$236,106	35%	65%	$82,637	$153,469
25 Disney	$1.3	$907,835	73%	27%	$662,720	$245,115
Rep -mil Republicans in millions						
19 Archer Dan. Mid.	Archer Daniels Midland					

Top supporters of the Republican Party for 2004

Company	Total	Dem	Rep	Dem	Rep
Wal-Mart	$2,008,101	19%	81%	$381,539	$1,626,562
United Parcel Services	$2,149,922	27%	73%	$580,479	$1,569,443
Price Waterhouse Coopers	$1,710,172	23%	77%	$393,340	$1,316,832
Ernst & Young	$1,814,290	36%	64%	$653,144	$1,161,146
Wachovia	$1,415,376	30%	70%	$424,613	$990,763
MBNA	$1,328,322	24%	74%	$318,797	$982,958
Pfizer	$1,402,127	33%	67%	$462,702	$939,425
FedEx Corp.	$1,316,571	32%	68%	$421,303	$895,268
General Electric	$1,651,262	46%	54%	$759,581	$891,681
Verizon	$1,444,096	40%	60%	$577,638	$866,458
AFLAC	$1,257,815	36%	64%	$452,813	$805,002
BellSouth	$1,363,749	42%	58%	$572,775	$790,974
Home Depot	$716,270	6%	94%	$42,976	$673,294
American Air/AMR 2002	$1,221,203	44%	55%	$537,329	$671,662
Wells Fargo	$1,046,967	36%	64%	$376,908	$670,059
General Motors	$899,041	31%	69%	$278,703	$620,338
Altria (Philip Morris)	$912,927	35%	65%	$319,524	$593,403
Ford	$729,084	28%	72%	$204,144	$524,940
Clear Channel	$764,318	33%	67%	$252,225	$512,093
Enterprise Rent-A-Car	$579,575	14%	86%	$81,141	$498,435
ExxonMobil	$550,717	12%	88%	$66,086	$484,631
Qwest	$750,912	36%	64%	$270,328	$480,584
AT&T	$644,069	48%	52%	$309,153	$334,916
American Airlines	$521,964	36%	64%	$187,907	$334,057
ChevronTexaco	$390,081	17%	83%	$66,314	$323,767
Disney	$907,835	73%	27%	$662,720	$245,115
Alticor/Amway	$238,788	0	100%	$0	$238,788
PepsiCo	$262,199	34%	66%	$89,148	$173,051
BP Amoco	$236,106	35%	65%	$82,637	$153,469

2004 Campaign Donors - Oil Companies

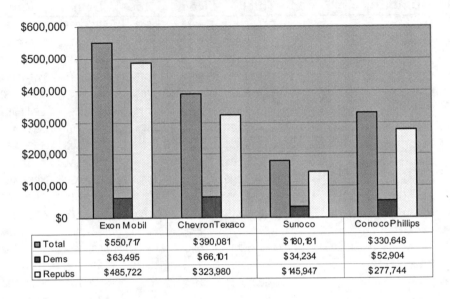

	Exon Mobil	ChevronTexaco	Sunoco	ConocoPhillips
Total	$550,717	$390,081	$180,181	$330,648
Dems	$63,495	$66,101	$34,234	$52,904
Repubs	$485,722	$323,980	$145,947	$277,744

2004 Campaign Donors - Oil Co's

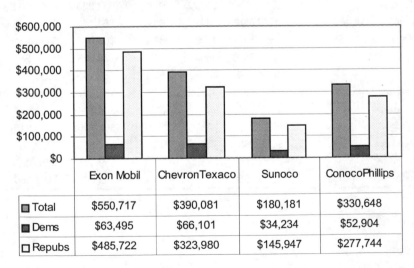

	Exon Mobil	ChevronTexaco	Sunoco	ConocoPhillips
Total	$550,717	$390,081	$180,181	$330,648
Dems	$63,495	$66,101	$34,234	$52,904
Repubs	$485,722	$323,980	$145,947	$277,744

A
nti-war groups are already boycotting some of these supporters. But a missing target, for whom a boycott would be most effective is the credit

card company, MBNA. The credit card market is very competitive judging by the number of credit card solicitations I receive everyday. They are begging me to dump my present card company and join them at incredibly attractive rates. In that climate, now is the perfect time to boycott MBNA credit card company. You can dump MBNA, transfer your balance and save money too. Can you imagine the impact if we set a specific date to drop MBNA cards and on that specified date MBNA receive over a million cancelled cards in the mail?

The goodwillie objective of this boycott of MBNA and other supporters of this war-mongering Republican Party is twofold:

Not another penny to the warmongering Republican Party until the US occupation of Iraq is abandoned.

At least 50% of the savings from cessation of financial support of Republicans be diverted to the creation of a "Margaret Hassan Memorial Fund to continue the volunteer work in Iraq for which Margaret Hassan gave her life.

The martyrdom of Margaret Hassan?

Margaret Hassan was a Dublin-born charity worker who lived in Iraq for over 30 years. She was married to an Iraqi engineer. She worked for Care International, the world's largest international humanitarian relief agency. The former Margaret Fitzsimmonds had Irish, British and Iraqi nationality. She had been on the ground helping the poor in Iraq for over 25 years. Hassan pursued this noble mission through the 1991 war, the subsequent years of the embargo, the second US war and subsequent invasion. She earned the respect, admiration and adoration of the Iraqi people especially the children, who mobbed her wherever she encountered them. She was a harsh and very articulate critic of both US wars and the embargo against Iraq.

Hassan was kidnapped in Baghdad on October 19, 2004, when men dressed in police uniforms stopped her car as she was being driven to her office. That was the last time she was seen. However, Hassan did appear in three harrowing videos released by captors calling themselves merely "an armed Islamic group". It showed her being physically abused and begging for her life. Those pleas as well as pleas of many Iraqi organizations, Iraqi protestors who paraded with her picture and banners calling for her freedom and even notorious fugitive resistance leader Abu Musab al-Zarqavi, who himself admitted to beheading hostages before, were in vain. About four weeks later, American troops found her headless body in the town of Falluja. Many questions remain about who would kill a woman so popular amongst the Iraqis, and uncharacteristically no organized terrorist group claimed responsibility for her killing.

In the jungle, it is the weakest one in the herd of animals that falls easy prey. Another good boycott strategy is to pick off the weakest in this herd of war supporters. In this respect, American Airlines, which donated more money than any other airline, is a perfect target. They are reportedly on the edge of bankruptcy, but that did not prevent them from donating $1.62 million to the war mongering Republican Party.

The Goodwill Buying Revolution/ Which bad corporations to boycott?

So, the Goodwill Revolution is also a buying revolution. The war-mongering supporters and these bad corporations that exploit workers must be boycotted. However, these bad corporations make a killing on not only the exploitation of workers, but also on the ignorance and the acceptance of consumers of this exploitation. Ignorance in this information age will be dispelled and I am counting on the basic goodness of people to join the boycott enthusiastically in their millions. We will be up against paid propagandist advertisers to deceive and obstruct this Goodwill Buying Revolution. They are professional and very expert at deception with their slick never-ending ads and high paid accomplices in the media, but I am confident in the goodness of people to prevail over the desire to save a badly tainted buck.

Dispelling Ignorance by becoming *coo-operators*

How do we find these bad eggs? Thanks to the internet, there are many organisations that rate companies or are urging boycotts. Sometimes their numbers are so large that they can be overwhelming and defeat their purpose. So the Goodwill Revolution will not come up with a new rating system but network with some of the existing organisations which do an excellent job.

One of the best is Co-Op America. Their website is invaluable. You have heard of a cool operator. Well Goodwillies are urged to become *coo-operators* by joining Co-Op America and be sure to use their Reliable Shopper http://www.responsibleshopper.org/ This is a very impressive guide to evaluating hundreds of companies on a range of issues, including: Sweatshops, Pollution, Ethics, Discrimination and more. It contains a huge database of companies which you can search on the basis of keywords, such as brand name or the name of the companies themselves.

Besides, another source of information will be the companies themselves. Just as they advertise bargain prices today, they will entice our bucks with advertising of the goodwillie changes they have made. Already some companies try to use advertising to tell us how good they are. Phillip Morris' advertising tell us about their great efforts to keep kids from smoking their cigarettes. Such efforts are commendable but we must be on guard to make sure that claims like that are true.

For example, Wal-Mart has all sorts of advertisements claiming the wonderful things that they are doing for their employees, their community and their country. This is a smokescreen and we have to be vigilant against being bamboozled by deceitful corporations.

Greenwashing is a good example of how deceitful corporations are. The Concise Oxford English Dictionary defines greenwashing as the *"disinformation disseminated by an organization so as to present an environmentally responsible public image."* It is what corporations do when they try to make themselves look more environmentally friendly than they really are. It is propaganda. They make deliberately misleading claims.

Numbers

Boycotts are dime a dozen. Why should the goodwillie boycott be any different? Numbers is the key. We have numbers, millions of potential goodwillies. An estimated ten million people worldwide, many braving freezing weather, marched to oppose the Iraq war that cold February morn in 2002. Months later millions marched to protect women's lives. But we failed to prevent the Iraq war and the war monger was re-elected. Now he spreads his tentacles over more national and world institutions by appointing fellow warmongers to head organizations like the World Bank. Women's lives are threatened more than ever before. If these millions join the Goodwill Revolution boycott we could reverse these losses and win.

Besides, these millions are just the tip of the iceberg. There are also millions who are dismayed at the victimization of the working man, the relentless attacks on unions to deprive workers of their rights as well as many other injustices that are flourishing these days. Many of us feel dispirited, frustrated, helpless and hopeless at the way many of our leaders have knuckled under and have betrayed us by their silence and inaction.

The many boycotts that exist now have failed to reach enough people. We need to network with the many organizations with goodwill as our common link and create a database of millions. Once upon a time, such a database would seem like fantasy, but technology will work for us. With the internet that goal is very feasible. So the goodwillie boycott is not just another boycott but is a call for individuals and these many organizations all over the world to work together on a joint boycott. With a database of boycotting millions, we will not be helpless anymore and we will be heeded.

But in order to achieve success, just as the Montgomery Alabama Bus Boycott we goodwillies must:

- Be organized
- Have a sense of purpose
- Persevere (the Montgomery Alabama bus boycott took over a year of sacrifice)
- Maintain solidarity
- Be resourceful, innovative and creative
- Be informed
- Be vigilant for deception

Goodwill Boycott techniques
- Boycott pledge – a signed pledge by individuals to join the boycott, why and for how long unless the company makes change before the time period.
- Letter to company before the boycott goes into effect with copy to congressperson

- Network boycott with organizations Co-op America, Global Exchange, Jobs With Justice, ANSWER , Move-On, with one or more of them taking lead in organising
- Create database of pledgies (a pledgie is anyone who signs the pledge) – the goodwillie aim is for a minimum of 1 million pledgies
- Set conditions company must meet to call off the boycott
- Time period for boycott after which conditions will be reviewed to decide whether to discontinue, continue or to switch boycott to a competitor
- Play one vs the other like Coke vs Pepsi (take advantage of product wars such as cola wars, burger wars)
- Provisional boycott where product is bought only if price drops to a substantially lower designated limit. (below profit level)
- Publicity for boycott campaign
- Boycott flexibility such as a one-day-per-week boycott depending on circumstances

United we boycott

The goodwillie boycott will be just another boycott unless it can unite a number of groups to join together to achieve success. Currently there are hundreds of groups which although they have a specific focus, really have objectives which are generally to achieve goodwill. For example, there are anti-war groups, unions, workers' rights groups, Democratic Clubs, the greens, progressive organizations, environmental organizations, human rights groups, civil rights groups and all sots of similar groups that would be our natural allies. Another thing that these groups have in common is that they are losing the battle. We will continue to lose the battle unless we unite, and not just unite, but unite with a winning plan. The boycott is that winning plan and we need to unite around it.

The first step is to form a working committee composed of members of about seven of these prominent groups with the resources to handle organization. I think some dynamic

experienced organisations which should be invited to join that organizing committee should include Co-op America, Global Exchange, Jobs With Justice, ANSWER and Move-On.
The duties of this committee would be to:
- Enlist other groups
- Create the data base of millions whether it be one data base or a daisy link chain of data bases but the data must be organized so that decisions, instructions and similar information may be shared with all virtually immediately.
- Decide on companies to boycott and boycott procedures like how and duration, etc..
- Monitor these companies for change to ensure accurate current information
- Publicity campaign
- Compose and send letters to companies giving them advance notice that they are potential targets for boycott of millions. Here is a sample letter:

Boycott Letter to Companies
Dear Sir,
On behalf of the Goodwill Revolution I am informing you that we are considering boycotting your company. We are in the process of unifying over a hundred organizations resulting in millions of members united in our fight for goodwill towards all and against injustice. We are horrified at the
- atrocious Iraq war
- the relentless attack on the rights of the working man
- the hiring of union busters
- the lack of a living wage
- the inadequacy of health benefits for workers
- other miscellaneous injustices
George Bush and his Republican Party launched the abominable illegal war against the people of Iraq and we are morally compelled to boycott the top financial supporters of this war-mongering

Republican Party. Judging by your continued
support of this war-mongering party by your
company and the other top supporters despite the
fact that:

- Over 100,000 Iraqi's have been killed.
- Two thousand pound bombs have been dropped
  on residential neighborhoods.
- We have used torture and human degradation.
- Water supply systems have been deliberately
  and systematically destroyed forcing the
  people to drink dirty and unsanitary water.
- Iraqis face 70% unemployment
- And so on

We must include your company for boycott.
We are also boycotting companies which have been
exploiting and victimizing the workers as
identified above. Please be warned that we will
not be bribed by lower prices.
All these companies will be considered for
boycott, but we think it is more effective to
concentrate on prime candidates. We think it will
take about six weeks to unite our forces for the
boycott and decide on the prime candidates from
the list which includes your company.
One of our tactics is when there are two
companies in the same sector, we will pick the
worse of the two to boycott and support the
other. I think it is called playing one against
the other. Considering this, if there is any new
improvement in your policies, please let us know
before we make a decision.
We are in this boycott for the long haul. It will
last for two years or until the conditions below
are met. After two years, we will review
conditions and decide whether to continue the
boycott or switch to another company in your
sector.
I think our demands are fair and reasonable and
they are as follows:

....

Be Committed/Personal commitment
The role of the individual is so important. Unlike other activities, action is not passed off to some official of an organization or some politician. It is up to us individuals to take direct action. For individuals it is not even necessary to spend money to join this Goodwill Buying Revolution. All you need to do is:
- Provide your email address for the database of millions
- Sign the boycott pledge
- Follow the boycott guidelines
- Help spread the word about the boycott

Publicity
Many a boycott has failed because of lack of publicity so we should not make that mistake. Downloadable brochures, bumper stickers, distribution of leaflets, letters to the editor and even advertising and other traditional PR measures should not be overlooked.

Boycott stocks too
But the bastion of the power of these corporations is the stock market. Most of us have not paid much attention to this aspect. But, not anymore. We will no longer be unwitting accomplices with them in profiting from their exploitation by buying their stock. *I, myself, would rather put my money in a mattress!* So, the same criteria we use to boycott their products we should also use to boycott their stocks.
A high rate of return on our money investment at low risk is nice, but not from these employee-exploiting-union busting corporations. There are many other equally profitable stocks out there. Don't let insensitive financial advisers or stock brokers tell you otherwise, which many are inclined to do. Most of them gave us a bum steer on our investments in the nineties stock market disaster anyhow. We followed their advice then only to be bamboozled by World.com, Global Crossing, Enron, accountants Arthur Anderson and others. So many of us saw our life savings decimated in that market collapse.

We have choices. That's the good thing about capitalism. We are not in the dark anymore. Thanks to the Internet we can get information to make the right choices. Two excellent sources of such information on the web are:

1. SocialFunds.com
    http://www.socialfunds.com/sa/index.cgi
2. Social Investment Forum, http://www.socialinvest.org/

We will seek these exploiting corporations out, whether in common stocks, or nestled in 401K or other mutual funds and take prudent divestment action.

Shareholder activism

But divestment is not the only action. Socially responsible investing also encompasses shareholder activism. Instead of divesting, these shareholders become active in the company. As shareholders, even with only a single share, they are entitled to raise issues on company policies and do. So, these activists can take the battle on social issues from right inside the belly of the corporate beast.

Reality check

We have no illusions. We know full well that as individual investors we are insignificant. But we Goodwillies will swell the ranks of the army of socially responsible investors already there to boycott these bad corporations.

The army of socially responsible investors is growing. In 1999, $1 out of every $8 invested in stocks was prompted by a socially conscious decision. That comes to $2.16 trillion of the $16.3 trillion professionally managed in the United States, or 13%. The $2.16 trillion figure is up 82% from 1997. Yet in 1984, there were only 40 billion dollars in socially responsible investing.

It is an uphill struggle, and we can prevail. But for sure, the Goodwill revolution will send a message that "*it won't be business as usual anymore*".

Chapter 15
Wal-Mart Sucks!

Wal-Mart is huge. Wal-Mart is powerful. Wal-Mart sucks! Walmart is a prime candidate for Montgomery-Alabama-bus-boycott treatment.

Boycott Wal-Mart
"You can lead a horse to Wal-Mart but you can't make him buy."
"Wal-Mart is coming! Wal-Mart is coming! Lock up your daughters!" Actually your daughters are safe but nothing strikes terror in the hearts of local retailers as the news that Wal-Mart is coming to their area. They know full well it is the death of their business and the death of most retail business in a 50 mile radius especially in small towns. But the 50 mile radius has shrunk. The net of Wal-Mart stores has become tighter as the number of stores have multiplied. Knocking aside zoning regulations, these massive aircraft-hangar looking stores have sprung up where no there stores have gone before. Recently one sprung up in the shadow of the Great Pyramid in Mexico to the dismay of environmentalists and history buffs. But, the Mexican consumers loved it.

Yes, Wal-Marts have spread from the sleepy south to encompass all of America and continues to take in country after country all over the world. It has become the largest retailer in the world. But, Wal-Mart is an evil empire. But not to consumers, as they pile into their cars, and choke the sprawling Wal-Mart parking lots in vast numbers in search of bargains as if they were the Holy Grail. But Wal-Mart is no Holy Grail. It is an evil empire that achieves its low prices on the callous exploitation of workers, exportation of American jobs to slave wage China, and an array of unfair business practices.

- Low wages
- Expensive health insurance
- Rabidly anti-union involved in union busting
- More disability discrimination suits against it than any other company

- More sexual discriminations against women employees suits
- Violations of workers compensation, child labor, surveillance of employees (over 1400 violations in Maine alone)

Besides, Wal-Mart gives more money to warmongering Republican candidates than any other company. Its top three managers, including its chief executive, donated the individual maximum $2,000 to President George W Bush. Its vice-president for corporate affairs, raised at least $100,000 to re-elect the president.

Wal-Mart and its millionaire apologists get on TV to justify employee exploitation by claiming that they are just being competitive to bring savings to consumers. It's more likely to enrich its owners and enrich its owners it has. Wal-Mart had sales of $259 billion for fiscal 2004. Of the ten richest people in the world, five are Waltons, heirs of the company founder now deceased, Sam Walton.

Their competitor COSTCO does not follow that low road of employee exploitation like Wal-Mart as :

- they pay their employees a living wage
- offer low health insurance premium that workers can afford
- instead of union busting workers are unionized with Teamsters in what is described as the "best retail contracts" in the US

Nevertheless, Wal-Mart's shoddy practices gives it an unfair advantage and it could force other retailers to follow suit and some already have. Wal-Mart needs to be rehabilitated! It is mainly because of these practices why it has grown to the world's number one retailer. These are just some of the policies which have also caused it to grow to number one most boycotted company in the world. Wal-Mart and others like Wal-Mart are counting on us to disregard these abuses for the sake of money, saving money. But for even someone on a fixed income, boycotting Wal-Mart is easy. Most of the buying there is impulse buying anyway. Retail stores go out of business all the time. Just consider Wal-Mart out of business, act like it does not exist anymore and move on.

For more information read Jim Hihghtower's wonderful article *"Boycott Wal-Mart, Why you should wipe that smiling yellow face of your shopping list."*

As Jim Hightower sums up, *"The bottom line is that Wal-Mart shrinks our economy, destroys middle-class wages, changes the face of our communities, and erodes America's values of fairness, justice, and opportunity. It's time to free the market again."*

Boycott Objective

To free the market again, Wal-Mart should be boycotted until it makes the following list of changes:

- Certification and cooperation with the union for the mutual betterment of the worker and company.
- Fire its union busters and replace them with union liason experts
- Living wage minimum for employees
- Putting pressure on suppliers in China and other foreign countries to upgrade wages and working conditions of workers there too
- Working with competitors to form an agreement to upgrade worker benefits
- Working to increase health benefits for employees by lowering premiums and making eligibility requirements easier
- Publicly supporting national health care for all.

"No more will corporation advertisers tell us what to buy. If anything we will tell them what to sell. We have lost our voting power so now we will use our buying power. They suppressed our voting power but they cannot suppress our buying power."

So price and quality are not the only criteria we need to use in shopping anymore. As a result of the Goodwill Buying Revolution we need to use additional criteria such as:

- Not a financial supporter of the war-mongering Republican Party
- Union product
- Environment friendly
- Living wage
- Social consciousness
- Community involvement and re-investment
- Equal opportunity
- Ratio of wages of highest paid employee to lowest no greater then 100 to 1

If years ago people of goodwill had refused to buy things produced by slave labor, slavery might have ended much sooner. Our boycott was instrumental in ending apartheid in South Africa. The Goodwill Revolution boycott is the only real hope of saving democracy. Join it.

Chapter 16
Goodwillies Everywhere

As my plane touched down in Montego Bay Jamaica, I had mixed feelings. Elated to be back home after more than 10 years if even for just one week. But, apprehensive, for immediately ahead were picking up my rental car and driving the length of the island, a very unnerving prospect. Away for over ten years, but not driven in Jamaica for over 20 years. Memories of narrow roads, driving on the left, sharing the road with careless reckless pedestrians and worst of all aggressive impolite drivers, dominated my memory of driving in Jamaica. I dreaded it. A half an hour later in my rental car I found my first challenge – making a right turn (equivalent to a left turn in the US) on to a major highway from a side street. Seeing a steady stream of traffic, I became resigned to an eternal wait to get on the main highway. Then I noticed the traffic backing up. "Great...just what I need. I'll never get in ". I thought. Then I realized why the traffic was backing up. They had stopped to let me in! A driver was furiously waving me in. This was completely unexpected by me. But it was not unique as all along my journey I encountered conspicuously polite considerate drivers. My memory owed those drivers an apology.

But a funny thing happened when I came back to the US. Suddenly I kept running into the same thing there – very polite considerate drivers! Where were they before my trip to Jamaica? They were always there. It's just that I did not notice them. So one of the best results of my trip to Jamaica was the altered perspective. I am very aware now of the many courteous drivers and I can really appreciate them. There is reason for optimism for the Goodwill Revolution. There are goodwillies everywhere. Unfortunately, they often go unnoticed and unappreciated, but that will change.

Then there are those whose lives have inspired the goodwill revolution. We are bombarded with PR for idolizing people for their athletic, musical, acting and especially their buck-making prowess. The 'Donald' and the rest of these become heroes and role models. But, our real heroes are ordinary people who do extraordinary things, extraordinarily good things. Two of these are Rachel Corrie and Ben Linder.

Rachel Corrie

Rachel Corrie gave her life doing good. She was killed Sunday, March 16, 2003, in the southern Gaza city of Rafah while trying to stop an Israeli bulldozer from tearing down a Palestinian physician's home.

Rachel grew up in Olympia, Washington. She was the daughter of Craig Corrie, an insurance executive, and Cindy Corrie, a school volunteer and flutist. She went to Evergreen State College, where she studied the arts and international relations.

During her college years, Rachel joined the Olympia Movement for Justice and Peace (*http://www.omjp.org/*) and participated in various peace and environmental activities. Later, she chose a very special and unique role. It takes additional and exceptional bravery to leave the comfort and confines of your own group, to support the cause of another outside group, one which is unpopular with your own group. But she had that type of exceptional bravery. So, even though she was Jewish, in her senior year she took a leave of absence to participate in the International Solidarity Movement (ISM). There she organized peaceful demonstrations against the Israeli occupation of Palestine and worked to initiate a sister city project between her hometown Olympia and the Palestinian city of Rafah.

The ISM, itself, was founded in 2001 by Adam Shapiro, a New York Jew, and his wife Huwaida Arraf, a Palestinian Christian along with the Israeli peace activist Neta Golan. The organisation recruits civilians from Western countries to participate in accompaniment and acts of non-violent resistance against the Israeli occupation of the West Bank, the Gaza Strip and East Jerusalem.

So to Rafah she came with other brave volunteers. The Palestinian children came to love her. She lived with their families and experienced their pain and victimization. But that day in march she stood in front of the bulldozer.She was opposing the demolition of not just that house, but the hundreds of houses demolished and the hundreds of families of men, women and children left homeless. This slender idealistic girl of a mere 23 was also opposing the world apathy of this blatant UN violation. The bulldozer crushed her skull.

She too wanted to live. In her own words reported by her mother from an email,

"…. *I really want to dance around to Pat Benatar and have boyfriends and make comics for my co-workers. But I also want this to stop. Disbelief and horror is what I feel. Disappointment. I am disappointed that this is the base reality of our world and that we, in fact, participate in it. This is not at all what I asked for when I came into this world. This is not at all what the people here asked for when they came into this world. This is not what they are asking for now. This is not the world you and Dad wanted me to come into when you decided to have me."*

We goodwillies have got to make this and all other types of injustice stop.

Ben Linder

Ben Linder wanted his life to make a difference. He wanted to make a significant contribution to the neediest and was doing just that in Nicaragua until a CIA trained contra terrorist took that life away.

Benjamin Ernest Linder (July 7, 1959—April 28, 1987), born in California, was a young American engineer who was killed in an ambush on April 28, 1987, by a group of CIA-funded Contras while working on a small hydroelectric dam that was to bring electricity and running water to a village in the middle of Nicaragua's war zone.

He graduated in 1983 with a degree in mechanical engineering from the University of Washington. Upon graduation, he did not seek to join up with a big war profiteering firm like Bechtel and earn massive bucks. Instead he immediately left his comfortable home in Oregon to live and work among the poor in Managua, Nicaragua. He developing and built small hydroelectric plants bringing electricity to villages in northern Nicaragua for the first time.

But he was not just an engineer. To the poor kids robbed of most joy in their lives by poverty, he was their pied piper. He took them away from that bitter reality by dressing up as a clown and entertaining them by riding his unicycle and juggling.

In 1986, Linder moved from Managua to El Cuá, a village in the Nicaraguan war zone, where he helped form a team to build a hydroplant to bring electricity to the town. Linder and two Nicaraguans -- Sergio Hernández and Pablo Rosales -- were killed in the Contra ambush while working at the construction site for a new dam for the nearby village of San José de Bocay. The autopsy showed that Linder was first wounded by a grenade, then shot at point-blank range in the head. The two Nicaraguans were also murdered at close range, Rosales by a stab wound in the heart.

Ben wrote, "*I see the kids and I feel like taking them all away to a safe place to hide until the war stops and the hunger stops and El Cuá becomes strong enough to give them the care they deserve. The pied piper of El Cuá. But I can't do that, and even if I could it wouldn't help the neighboring towns. So instead, I try to put in light, and hope for the best.*"

A bullet from a CIA-funded contra terrorist did put his light out. But that light will forever burn in our hearts and memory and inspire goodwillies to light up the world with their own good deeds.

Not only are there goodwillies everywhere, but there are also goodwillie organizations everywhere. These organizations tap into the natural goodness of mankind, so that Shakespeare's evaluation rings true.

"What a piece of work is a man! How noble in reason! how infinite in faculty! in form, in moving, how express and admirable! in action how like an angel! in apprehension how like a god! the beauty of the world! the paragon of animals!" Hamlet. Act I. Scene II.

These organizations abound. Happily, they are too numerous to mention and they cover such a wide scope. But here is a sample of a few:

Doctors Without Borders

The story is told which I readily admit I am unable to authenticate about this person who dies and goes up to heaven. As soon as he meets St. Peter he exclaims that he would like to meet the Virgin Mary more than anything else. St. Peter obliges, so he gets his life wish, to meet the Virgin Mary. He greets her with much enthusiasm, effusion and of course admiration which he makes no attempt to conceal. So he beamed, " *At last, the Virgin Mary, the mother of Jesus, the mother of God! The mother of a god! You must be so proud of your son, a god!*" To which Mary replies, " *Ahhhh I would rather he were a doctor.* "

Doctors do enjoy high prestige in the upper echelons of our society. Typically they lead a life of luxury and epitomize material success. But, a rare group of doctors have turned their back on this easy living to venture into foreign lands racked by disaster either natural or even worse, the man-made kind such as wars, to help by bringing medical relief to the victims. These brave dedicated doctors belong to Medicins Sans Frontieres (MSF) known in english as Doctors Without Borders which has delivered emergency aid from Chechnya to Angola , from Kosovo to war devastated Iraq. Yes, they have served and risked their lives even in Iraq until November 2003. They had to pull out as it was just too dangerous.

MSF was founded in 1971 by a small group of French doctors who believed that all people have the right to medical care regardless of race, religion, creed or political affiliation, and that the needs of these people supersede respect for national borders. It was the first non-governmental organization to both provide emergency medical assistance and publicly bear witness to the plight of the populations they served.

This private non-profit volunteer organization unites direct medical care with a commitment to bearing witness and speaking out against the underlying causes of suffering. Its volunteers protest violations of humanitarian law on behalf of populations who have no voice, and bring the concerns of their patients to public forums, such as the United Nations, governments (in both home and project countries), and the media. In a wide range of circumstances, MSF volunteers have spoken out about forgotten conflicts and underreported atrocities they have witnessed, including Iraq.

But MSF is not only doctors. It is an international network with sections in 18 countries. Each year, more than 2,500 volunteer doctors, nurses, other medical professionals, logistics experts, water/sanitation engineers, and administrators join 15,000 locally hired staff to provide medical aid in more than 80 countries.

MSF has built a strong logistical capability to support its medical expertise, enabling its volunteers to work in the most remote or unstable parts of the world.

At the onset of emergencies, teams arrive at a project site with prepackaged medical kits so they can begin working immediately. Custom-designed by MSF for specific field situations, geographic conditions, and climates, a kit may contain a complete surgical theater, or all the supplies needed to treat hundreds of cholera patients. MSF kits have been replicated by relief organizations worldwide. With such impressive feats, it is no wonder that MSF won the Nobel Peace Prize in 1999.

Responsible Wealth

Responsible Wealth is a group that defies the mean greedy stereotype of the rich. This group does not consist of your average joes, but is comprised of the wealthiest 5% of Americans, the primary beneficiaries of the robust growth of the American economy. Responsible Wealth is a national network of businesspeople, investors and affluent Americans who are concerned about deepening economic inequality and are working to make prosperity more widespread. They are leaders in business, community, government, philanthropy, academia and finance.

Their three main areas of work are:

1. Tax fairness - Since 1998, hundreds of their wealthy members have protested tax cuts for the affluent by taking the "Tax Fairness Pledge" in which they formally pledge to give the proceeds of their annual tax cuts – over $3 million so far – to support groups that organize for a fair tax system and real economic justice. They also oppose the repeal of the estate

tax, which would be an windfall exclusively for the richest 2% of taxpayers.

2. Living wage- here again they formally pledge to pay their own employees a living wage and to publicly support its adoption to Members of Congress, peers including investment advisors, and mutual fund managers, management of stock companies, among civic groups, religions organizations and local newspapers. And, like goodwillies they encourage members to patronize business that pay a living wage.

3. corporate responsibility - they call for greater corporate accountability.

Jobs With Justice

One of the most endangered species today is the union worker. The only obstacle to big business and the complicity of powerful politicians steamrolling workers' rights is the union. So, the union needs help. It cannot depend on its battered and besieged members alone. Jobs With Justice (JwJ) is the cavalry.

Jobs with Justice is a coalition of labor organizations, community groups and thousands of individual activists dedicated to protecting the rights of working people and supporting community struggles to build a more just society. JwJ mobilizes support for labor and community struggles at rallies, on picket lines, in educational settings and at meetings and hearings. The basic building block of JwJ is a pledge that people sign to turn out to support other people's struggles at least five times a year.

They give critical support through these coalitions which now exist in over 40 cities in 29 states all over the US. Not only do they defend vigorously the basic right of workers to organize, join a union and collectively bargain but they also work for:

- Health care for all
- Global justice: highlighting the domestic impacts of globalization and fostering international solidarity among workers and communities around the world.
- Immigrant rights: denouncing attacks on immigrant workers and communities.

Washington DC Jewish Community Council

Christmas is a very important time for the Washington DC Jewish Community Center (DCJCC). This might seem surprising since the center, as expected, is designed primarily to preserve and strengthen Jewish identity, heritage, tradition, and values through a wide variety of social, cultural, recreational, and educational programs and services. But, Christmas day has special meaning there. Since Christmas is not a holiday for Jews, the DCJCC takes advantage of the perfect opportunity to help bring cheer to others in the community. It fulfils the strong Jewish tradition of Tikum Olam, helping to repair the world.

So every year on December 25th, the center recruits and organizes over 1,500 volunteers to serve meals to the homeless, entertain seniors and poor children, give blood, paint the community center walls, gives out donated toys, gloves, hats, scarves, socks and toiletries collected beforehand to hundreds of homeless and other needy people. In all about sixty different volunteer activities will go on all day, beginning at 6 a.m.

This project serves three purposes: it provides companionship and a more joyful holiday for the needy, respite for over-worked staff at more than 60 social service agencies, and something very meaningful to do for those who don't necessarily celebrate the holiday.

ACORN

ACORN, the Association of Community Organizations for Reform Now, is the nation's largest community organization of low and moderate-income families, with over 175,000 member families organized into 850 neighborhood chapters in 73 cities across the country. Their priorities include: better housing for first time homebuyers and tenants, living wages for low-wage workers, more investment in their communities from banks and governments, and better public schools. They achieve these goals by building community organizations that have the power to win changes -- through direct action, negotiation, legislation, and voter participation. It was founded by Wade Rathke in 1970 and the first membership was a group of Arkansas welfare mothers. ACORN's first priority is building organization in low-income communities. Major campaigns, whether around housing, or jobs, or voter registration, are designed to reach the unorganized majority of low and moderate-income people - the key constituency that must be mobilized for a progressive movement for social change in this country to succeed.

Acorn has a strong active immigrant membership base. This has motivated ACORN to begin a new international program to build strategic partnerships with grassroots organizations in other countries. Through these partnerships, ACORN will help to strengthen democratic movements for social change abroad, while continuing its efforts building power for immigrant communities in the United States.

ACORN International's priority is to build grassroots partnerships in countries from which they have significant immigrant membership communities. ACORN International's programs will seek not only to sustain grassroots organizing in these countries, but also to build the local-global connections between their members in the United States and low-income communities fighting for social justice abroad. Cross-border issues that affect these communities include the costly fees banks charge to send remittances, predatory lending and immigration policies. So far rhey have established overseas offices in Peru, the Dominican Republic and Canada.

Projects of Hope/ Seeds of Peace and the Ulster Project

To really heal the world, one has to heal the many rifts in the world. There are organizations that are already using goodwill to heal these rifts. A couple of these rifts are the conflict between Israelis and Palestinians and between Protestants and Catholics in Northern Ireland. Rifts that have gone on for generations and seems like they will go on to generations yet unborn. Hopes have been dashed. Politicians have failed. But organizations of hope have stuck their necks out to rescue new generations of potential antagonists from conflict.

Two of these rift healer organizations are the Seeds of Peace and the Ulster Project. Both organizations remove kids from each of the warring sides in their strife-torn native lands and bring them to America. There they live with each other and American kids.

Seeds of Peace creates a total coexistence experience at a summer camp in Maine in which Arab and Israeli teenagers live, play, learn, eat and sleep together. This intensive, month-long program combines recreational sports and arts activities with daily conflict-resolution sessions led by professional American, Arab and Israeli facilitators. Through the coexistence workshops, participants develop empathy, respect, communication/negotiation skills, confidence and hope - the building blocks for peaceful coexistence.

Founded in 1993 by author and journalist John Wallach, Seeds of Peace has intensified its impact with each passing year, increasing the number of Middle East participants from 50 in 1993 to over 400 by 2004, and expanding the regional representation from two to eight nations. To date, over 1,500 Israeli , Palestinian, Egyptian, Jordanian, Moroccan, Tunisian, Qatar, Yemeni, Cypriot, Greek, Turkish and Balkan teenagers have graduated from the program.

In the **Ulster Project**, equal number of pairs of Catholic and protestant teens are taken from Northern Ireland each year for a month. Instead of a camp, the teens live with host families in which Catholics live with Catholic host families and vice versa. They are also paired with American teenagers of the same sex and approximate age in each host family. During the month, the entire group of Northern Irish and American teens meet almost daily for activities, including encounter sessions, social activities, community service projects, and worship. These projects take place in many US cities and are sponsored and organized by churches both here in the US and in Northern Ireland.

The idea originated from a Church of Ireland (Anglican) priest, Canon Kerry Waterstone, a clergyman in Manchester, Connecticut, based on his personal experience with his own kids. Canon Waterstone felt that the attitudes of teenagers from Northern Ireland might be changed, so as to influence the future in Northern Ireland, if they could see and experience the way Americans have learned to live together in their "melting-pot" society. So with the approval and cooperation of church leaders, the first Project got underway in 1975, and by 1995 there were 25 Projects here in the United States. By the end of 2002, over 6,100 youth from Northern Ireland have participated.

The project has been a remarkable success in which:

• The participants have been able to maintain their friendships with the support of the churches and neighborhood communities. Their influence extends to a large peer group, as well as their extended families.

• Parents of the Project youth have crossed sectarian lines in safety to work cooperatively on behalf of the Project.

• American teens and adults experience the joy of "hands-on" peacemaking, and lasting friendships that are made with the Northern Irish visitors and with other Americans.

• The Project has strengthened the ecumenical ties of cooperation among the churches of the various city Project locations.

This is goodwill in action. Both Seed for Peace and the Ulster Project show clearly how goodwill in action can overcome the most passionate and deep-seated of divisions and bring not just peaceful coexistence, but lasting friendship and generate even more goodwill.

Surfside – Portrait of a goodwillie town

In the shadows of the sprawling metropolis of Miami is the little seaside town of Surfside, population 4,500. It may be a little town, but it has a big heart. It is a place where the town hall often doubles as a depot of relief supplies destined for poverty stricken, storm-ravaged lands. It is a town that reaches out beyond its narrow borders, and beyond the borders of the USA to help people in need. It is a town of goodwill, a goodwill which it extended primarily to a battered country which really needed that goodwill, Haiti.

Paul Novak, as a six-time mayor of Surfside, mobilized the goodwill in his fellow residents to reach outside their comfort zones to help Haiti and others countries in need. He created Team Surfside, a team of volunteers, sponsored by the town and coordinated by its officials. Its original mission was to help local citizens to prepare, cope, and recover from hurricanes or other threats to their community.

In 1998 hurricane George threatened Surfside but hit Haiti instead. I need to mention :

- Haitians are black, but Surfside citizens are not
- Haiti is poor but Surfside citizens are not
- Haitians speak French, but Surfside citizens do not
- Some nearby Florida cities have a large Haitian population, but Surfside does not

Despite these obvious differences Team Surfside sprung into action. Preparations that they had made for Surfside hurricane relief was not needed. But, they were desperately needed in Haiti. So to Haiti , Team Surfside went.

Surfside's volunteers dispatched emergency relief teams, all volunteers paying their own expenses, with Mayor Novack leading the groups into desolate areas of Haiti.   At all of the stops, Team Surfside was out there as the only relief agency - there were no United Nations, no Red Cross, no other relief efforts underway at that time in those places. Supplies such as non-perishable food, drinking water, baby items, and clothes, along with other important recovery items such as shovels and hand tools were distributed directly to hurricane victims as a result of the cooperation and coordination between Surfside town officials, the volunteers of Team Surfside, and Mayors and local officials of communities in Haiti.

Since then, Mayor Novack and Team Surfside have also participated in relief efforts following disasters in the Dominican Republic, Honduras, and in El Salvador. Going beyond the provision of relief supplies, Surfside's volunteers have provided leadership and logistical training to municipal officials from Haiti and from other nations, enabling them to be of far greater short term and long term service to their cities, towns and communities.

Team Surfside have been recognized by the United States Southern Command, the Congressional Record of the United States, Voice of America Radio, National Public Radio, the Florida League of Cities, and by numerous elected officials at all levels of government including Presidents and Ambassadors of foreign nations.

After serving a record six terms, Paul Novack has given up his annual salary of $1, with no benefits and no pension, as mayor. He is no longer the mayor, but his legacy of goodwill lives on as Team Surfside stands ready today to offer their help to poor countries in need.

Other goodwillies

There are many others who have given up a life of comfort and even luxury to endure harsh poverty conditions abroad and even risking their lives too. There are those brave dedicated souls, who volunteered to be human shields against the bombs. From all over the world, they came to Iraq to help prevent the war by offering their bodies as shields against the bombs. Yes, there are lots of real heroes out there. While many other undeserving headline-grabbers get public adulation, these real heroes are unknown and unsung. But, they work on. They continue to do good deeds.

But, we are not asking goodwillies to do anything so drastic. You will not be asked to try to block home demolishing bulldozers in Rafah as Rachel Corrie did. All you will have to do is boycott. Surely if Rachel Corrie can give her life to do good, you can boycott companies that directly or indirectly support the vicious and illegal war against the people of Iraq. If a Ben Linder can leave his comfortable home and abandon a lucrative career to help the poor in the wilds of Nicaragua, surely you can boycott an employee- exploiting Wa-lmart. Think of Doctors Without Borders the next and every time hereafter you make out your shopping list.

The boycott's the thing!

The boycott's the thing. We have tried everything else. How many of you like me have done it all? For, yes, I have done it all I have:

- Handed out literature at shopping malls, grocery stores, concerts, county fairs and special festivals of all types
- Joined political organizations
- Served on special committees
- Moved resolutions
- Written my senator, congressperson, and all sorts of delegates
- Emailed my senator, congressperson, and all sorts of delegates

- Telephoned my senator, congressperson, and all sorts of delegates
- Marched in demonstrations and protest rallies
- Written numerous letters to editors
- Called in to radio talk shows
- Hosted talk show on radio
- Done extensive phone banking
- Signed millions of petitions
- Participated in all sort of worthy cause fundraisers
- Subscribed to all sorts of progressive and worthy organizations and campaigns

I have received lots of criticism for doing this. The most telling criticism is, " *You are wasting your time. You cannot make a difference!"* I wonder, but I always reply that I do what I can. To do nothing is not an option. Time for a new strategy and the boycott is the thing. If we put half the effort that we put in the activities above, we will be successful.

A successful boycott can make a difference. For a boycott to be successful, we need large numbers of people to commit to it. There are some who dismiss a boycott as ineffective. But not if we have the numbers. We have millions that feel the way we do. Millions have protested the war against Iraq. Millions of us who care feel frustrated, helpless and betrayed by our democracy. Millions of us are aghast as we see the corporations that exploit workers flourish and the reputable and fair corporations bite the dust. There are millions of goodwillies everywhere. But we need them to come in from the cold and join us in the Goodwill Revolution boycott of millions. Let us begin to build a database of millions. Let us network with organizations that care, all potentially goodwillie organizations to create that database of millions.

The goodwill revolution needs you. Let all these good deeds inspire you to join the goodwill revolution and make goodwill to all a way of life.

Two slogans which unfortunately reflect our times are "*Ask me if I care?"* and "*You mistook me for someone that gives a damn".* What an indictment of our society. But we see from the sample of these aforementioned persons and organizations that a lot of people care. Despite this increasing cynical culture, organizations like Doctors Without Borders and all these organizations project hope.

With goodwill towards all we can cut that big heavy dead albatross of materialism from around our necks,
- which made us do stupid things
- which made us do mean things
- which made us do selfish things
- which made us do evil things
- which made us do regrettable things.

With goodwill towards all we can help to build a world in which the big multinational corporations will voluntarily:
- unionize their employees in order to ensure their voice is heard and their rights protected
- make a living wage the minimum wage
- push and lobby for universal health care for all.

Now the world sucks, but with goodwill towards all, we can build a truly wonderful world.